THE PRIME FAMILY

NOTES

GENEALOGICAL, BIOGRAPHICAL
AND BIBLIOGRAPHICAL
OF THE

Prime
Family

BY

E. D. G. PRIME, D.D.

HERITAGE BOOKS
2020

HERITAGE BOOKS

AN IMPRINT OF HERITAGE BOOKS, INC.

Books, CDs, and more—Worldwide

For our listing of thousands of titles see our website
at
www.HeritageBooks.com

Published 2009 by
HERITAGE BOOKS, INC.
Publishing Division
100 Railroad Ave. #104
Westminster, Maryland 21157

International Standard Book Numbers
Paperbound: 978-0-7884-2679-7
Clothbound: 978-0-7884-7618-1

PREFATORY.

THESE Notes are printed, not for publication, but for more convenient preservation and reference, in one branch of the family to which they relate. They are dedicated by the compiler to the memory of his father, the REV. NATHANIEL SCUDDER PRIME, D.D., a man of rare intellectual endowments, an accomplished scholar, a faithful minister of the Gospel, a friend and active promoter of popular and liberal education, a fearless and uncompromising advocate of what he believed to be true and right. He left his impress upon the generation in which he lived, and especially upon the hearts of his children; one chief incentive in whose lives has been a desire to emulate his zeal in the acquisition and diffusion of useful knowledge, and to keep in honor his name by carrying out the principles and aims which he instilled into their minds.

E. D. G. P.

NEW YORK,
January 2, 1888.

CONTENTS.

THE PURITAN EXODUS.

THE earlier colonies of New England were appropriately called "Plantations." The seed was here sown which for two centuries and a half has been bearing fruit, not alone on this continent, but the world over. The full harvest has not yet been garnered, and will not be until the Son of Man shall send forth his reapers at the end of the world to gather the sheaves from the four quarters of the globe.

The story of the settlement of New England is a familiar one. It was the fruit of the spirit of persecution that prevailed in Old England in the sixteenth and seventeenth centuries. That spirit was kept alive during the reign of Henry VIII.; it burst into a flame under "the bloody Mary;" it was only partially suppressed in the days of Elizabeth; it broke out with fresh violence under James I. During these latter reigns many of whom England and the world were not worthy were driven from their native land to this Western wilderness, to seek a place where they might worship God according to the dictates of their own consciences, and the way was preparing for the greater exodus that took place under Charles I. Of the more than twenty thousand Puritans who left England for America before the opening of the Long Parliament in 1641, nineteen-twentieths emigrated during the period in which Charles I. held the royal sceptre, and Archbishop Laud the torch of persecution. Of this period the historian Bancroft says: "The pillory "had become the bloody scene of human agony and "mutilation as an ordinary punishment, and the friends "of Laud jested on the sufferings which were to cure "the obduracy of fanatics. They were provoked to the "indiscretion of a complaint, and then involved in a per- "secution. They were imprisoned and scourged; their "noses were slit; their ears were cut off; their cheeks "were marked with a red-hot brand. But the lash and "the shears and the glowing iron could not destroy "principles which were rooted in the soul, and which "danger made it glorious to confess."

Alarmed by the departure of so many whom it could ill afford to lose, though professing to despise their principles, the Government took active measures to prevent the increasing emigration. But the tide continued to flow out and to set irresistibly toward the New World, which was predestined as the land of freedom, — religious and civil.

Among those who left England during this period were JAMES and MARK PRIME, brothers. The latter joined the colony which settled the town of Rowley, Mass. From him was descended the family distinguished in the financial history of New York city in connection with the banking-house of Prime, Ward, and King. JAMES PRIME joined the colony that settled Milford, Conn. To him and to his descendants in one direct line the following records will be confined.

MILFORD PLANTATION.

MILFORD was one of the six independent settlements which were afterward united in what was known as the "Old Jurisdiction of New Haven." The colonies that formed this union were New Haven, Milford, Guilford, Branford, and Stamford in Connecticut, and Southold on Long Island. The main body of these colonists arrived in detachments in 1638, and made New Haven their common place of rendezvous; but they did not unite in any common government, nor did the several colonies join in any church relation. The majority of them remained at New Haven, waiting until they should decide on their respective locations. Either before leaving England, or while on the way hither, they had chosen for settlement the tract of land on Long Island Sound between the Connecticut River and the New York boundary, — a region which was still inhabited exclusively by Indians; but the precise locality of each colony had not been selected, except in the case of New Haven.

The land eventually chosen by the Milford Colony, situated about ten miles west of New Haven, was purchased of the Indians in the winter of 1638–39. The deed bears date Feb. 12, 1639, but the settlement was not begun until the following summer. On the 22d of August, 1639 (the day on which the church of New Haven was organized), the Milford church also was formed at the same place. As soon as the latter organization was completed, the colonists took up the line of march through the primeval forest, following an Indian trail by a devious route to the site of the present town of Milford. Arriving at their destination, they set up their banner in the name of the Lord, — a little company in a great wilderness, but a free and independent people, owning no allegiance, civil or religious, save to the King of kings, the Supreme Head of the Church.

At the first general meeting of the colonists, called "The General Court," it was voted "That they would "guide themselves in all their doings by the rule of the "written Word of God till such time as a body of laws "should be established."

At the same meeting it was voted "That the power "of electing officers and persons to divide the land into "lots, to take order for the timber, and to manage the "common interests of the Plantation, should be in the "church only; and that the persons so chosen should "be only from among themselves." Those who were thus exclusively invested by their church membership with the rights of citizenship in the colony were called "freemen." The Indian name of the place, Wepowaug, was retained until the meeting of the "General Court," Nov. 24, 1640, when it was changed to Milford. The earliest map of the colony known to exist, bearing date 1646, has, among the names of settlers and owners of lots designated, that of JAMES PRIME. He arrived at

Milford in 1644, coming, it is believed, from near Doncaster, Yorkshire, England, and being of Huguenot descent. The name was variously written in England, — Prime, Pryme, Preem, etc. In the early official records of Milford, James Prime is called "Freeman" and "Planter." He died in 1685, leaving a considerable estate, a minute inventory of which, including several tracts of land in and around Milford, personal property, household furniture, and farming implements, made out by appraisers and sworn to before R. Treat, governor, is on record in the Probate Court of New Haven County.

JAMES PRIME, of Milford Colony, left a son, JAMES PRIME, 2d, who, according to the family record, lived to be a hundred and three years and some months old. He died at Milford, July 18, 1736, his wife, Sarah, having died Aug. 20, 1721. He had three sons, James, Joseph, and EBENEZER; and seven daughters, Martha, Elizabeth, Sarah, Rebekah, Mary, Deborah, and Hannah. JAMES PRIME, 2d, was a large landholder, as appears from the town records of Milford, which contain thirty-four deeds of land executed by him during the period extending from 1686 to 1736, the year of his death. He was also one of the original proprietors of the township of New Milford, on the Housatonic River, which was purchased in 1702, and settled chiefly by families from Milford. He does not appear to have resided at New Milford at any time, but is set down in the records among the non-residents, on whom a special tax was levied for the building of the meeting-house and the support of the ministry. James Prime, 3d (son of James Prime, 2d), purchased the "Rights" of his father at New Milford, became a resident of that town, a deacon in the church, and the progenitor of a numerous branch of the family at that place and in the township of Washington, which was subsequently set off from New Milford by State enactment.[1]

The last will and testament of James Prime, 2d, of Milford, copied from the Records of New Haven County, is here given as a specimen of the legal documents of that period. It does not materially differ from the forms that are in use at the present day, but its personal features are interesting.

"LAST WILL & TESTAMENT OF JAMES PRIME, OF MILFORD, CONN.

"In the name of God Everlasting, Amen. This "23ᵈ day of September, in the Sixth yeare of yᵉ "Reigne of oʳ Sovereign Lord, George yᵉ Second, "King of Great Britain, Anno Dom. 1732, J, James "Prime of Milford, in yᵉ County of New Haven, in "His Majesty's Colony of Connecticut, in New Eng-

---

[1] In some of the New England settlements, after the first meeting-houses were built, one of the problems appears to have been to seat the people according to rank, so that all should be satisfied. At New Milford, for instance, Deacon James Prime was appointed on a committee to gather timber for the completion of the meeting-house, which had already been occupied in an unfinished state. When it was completed, the matter of seating the congregation came up. It was voted that "Dignity shall be allowed in the business; that the "highest seat is the pew next to the pulpit; the second is the forward "seat in the body of seats; the third is the hinder pew." It was then voted that "All men in this town that bear lists shall be first "seated in four ranks, according to tax-lists; then all that are 16 "years of age shall be seated according to their age; the widows "shall keep their seats; Mr. Samuel Brown's wife shall keep her "seat; and Deacon Prime's wife shall sit in the middle pew."

"land, Being arrived to Old Age & Being weak of
"Body but of Sound Mind & Memory (thanks be
"given unto God therefore), calling unto mind the
"Mortality of my Body, & knowing it is Appointed
"for man once to Dye, do Make & Ordain this my
"last Will & Testament; that is to say: Principally
"& first of all, J Give & Recommend my soul into
"ye Hands of God y^t Gave it, & my body J recom-
"mend unto ye Earth to be Buryed in decent & Chris-
"tian Buryall by my Executors, & at their Discretion,
"nothing doubting but at the General Resurrection
"I shall Receive ye same again by the Mighty power
"of God; & as touching my worldly Goods &
"Estate wherewith it has pleased God to bless me, J
"Give, Devise, & Dispose in the following manner
"& form, viz.: —

"Imp^r. My Will is that all my just Debts, Dues,
"& Demands y^t may be made upon my Estate & my
"Funerall charges be first Payd by my Ex^{rs}.

"Item. J Give, Dispose, & Bequeath to my daugh-
"ter Sarah Plumb the sum of One Hundred Pounds
"as money, to her & her heirs forever, to be paid
"out of my Estate by my Executors.

"Item. J Give, Dispose, & Bequeath to my eldest
"daughter Martha Prindle ye sum of One Hundred
"Pounds as money, to be paid to her out of my
"Estate by my Executors.

"Item. J Give, Dispose, & Bequeath to my daugh-
"ter Rebekah Clarke, & to her heirs forever, the
"sum of One Hundred Pounds as money, to be paid
"by my Executors out of my Estate.

"Item. J Give, Dispose, & Bequeath to my daugh-

" ter Mary Ford, & to her heirs forever, the sum of
" One Hundred Pounds as money, to be paid out of
" my Estate by my Executors.

" Item.   J Give, Dispose, & Bequeath to my daugh-
" ter Deborah Prime, & to her heirs forever, the sum
" of One Hundred Pounds as money, to be paid out
" of my Estate by my Executors.

" Item.   J Give & Bequeath unto my daughter
" Hannah Prime, & to her heirs forever, the sum of
" One Hundred Pounds as money, to be paid out of
" my Estate by my Executors.

" Item.   My Will is if either of my daughters y^t
" are not yet married shall dye before Marriage &
" without ifsue, y^e s^d Legacy given to y^e daughter y^t
" shall lodge shall be Equally Divided by the Sur-
" viving Children.

" Item.   J Give, Dispose, & Bequeath to my three
" sons, James Prime, Joseph Prime, & Ebenezer Prime,
" all the rest & remainder of my Goods & Estate,
" both Reall & Personall whatsoever, y$^·$ is not before
" Given & Disposed of by me, to them & their heirs
" & assignes forever, Equally to be divided, that is to
" say, to each of them y^e s^d James, Joseph, & Eben-
" ezer, one third part thereof, to them, their heirs &
" assignes forever.

" Item.   My Will is, & J do hereby Constitute &
" Nominate & Appoint my three sons, James Prime,
" Joseph Prime, & Ebenezer Prime, to be the only
" & sole Executors of this my last Will & Testament,
" & J do hereby dysanyull, revoke, & make void all
" other Testaments, Wills, Legacys, Bequests Exe-
" cuted by me anyways before made, namd, willd, &

" bequeathd. Ratefying & Confirming of this to be
" my last Will & Testament, J have hereunto sett my
" hand & affix^d my seal ye day & date first above
" written.

" JAMES PRIME, his ⎡ SEAL. ⎤

" Signed, Sealed, Published, & dec^d by James Prime
" as his last Will & Testament, in ye Presence of John
" Fowler, Ephraim Strong, John Gand.

" Proved, Milford, Sept. 6th, 1736."

REV. EBENEZER PRIME.

EBENEZER PRIME, third son of James Prime, 2d, and Sarah his wife, was born at Milford, Conn., July 21, 1700. He pursued his studies under the direction of his pastor, the Rev. Samuel Andrew, who was then acting-president of what afterward was known as Yale College. At the beginning of the last century there were only two collegiate institutions in the country, — Harvard in Massachusetts, and William and Mary in Virginia. In 1701 the Legislature of Connecticut chartered a collegiate school, which in the early diplomas was styled *Gymnasium Academicum*. It was nominally located at Saybrook, but for many years it waited on the convenience of its presiding officer. On the death of the first "rector," the Rev. Abraham Pierson, of Killingworth, in 1707, the Rev. Samuel Andrew, pastor at Milford, was chosen "rector *pro tempore*," and continued to discharge the duties of the position until the college was permanently located at New Haven in 1716.[1]

---

[1] Rev. Samuel Andrew (pronounced "one of the best scholars of his time") was fifty-two years pastor at Milford. He was born at Cambridge, Mass., Jan. 29, 1656, and was graduated at Harvard College in 1675. He was one of the projectors and founders of Yale College, was a trustee from the date of its charter until his death, thirty-six years, and rector, or president, *pro tempore* nine years. He

2

The senior class was under his immediate instruction at Milford, the lower classes being under tutors at Saybrook.

Ebenezer Prime was graduated in 1718,[1] when the first college building was completed at New Haven and inaugurated in time for holding the Commencement exercises within its walls. A history of the College says, " This Commencement was a memorable occasion, and " was celebrated in a style which far surpassed anything " known before in the history of the College." The name " Yale" was given to the new building in honor of the benefactor of the College, Governor Elihu Yale; it was not adopted as the corporate title of the institution until the year 1745, when a new charter was obtained from the Legislature.

After his graduation Mr. Prime began the study of divinity, — probably under his pastor, Mr. Andrew. In 1719, before he had completed his eighteenth year, he received an invitation from Huntington, Long Island, to become an assistant to the Rev. Eliphalet Jones, who was for nearly sixty years pastor of the church at that place. He accepted the invitation, and preached his first sermon at Huntington, June 21, 1719. After serving as assistant-minister four years, he was ordained and installed pastor, June 5, 1723.

The following records were made in the session-book

was one of the ministers who, by order of the General Court of Connecticut, met in synod at Saybrook in 1708 and adopted the manual of doctrine and discipline known as " The Saybrook Platform." He died at Milford, Jan. 24, 1737–8, aged eighty-two.

[1] Ebenezer Prime was two years in college with Jonathan Edwards, who was three years his junior in age, and two in graduation.

of the Presbyterian Church of Huntington by the hand
of the Rev. Ebenezer Prime : —

" My ordination to the Sacred Service of ye gospel
" ministry in Huntington was attended on June 5, 1723.
" The Reverend Presbyters that carried on ye solem-
" nity were :
  " Mr Eliphalet Jones, Huntington;
  " Mr Joseph Webb, Fairfield;
  " Mr Ebenezer White, Bridgehampton;
  " Mr Stephen Buckingham, Norwalk;
  " Mr Samuel Chapman, Greensfarm;
  " Mr Benjamin Woolsey, Southold.
  " The sermon was preached by the Rev. Mr. Chap-
" man, & the charge was given by the Rev. Mr. Jones
" in the following words : "

Here follows the charge, copied in full.

" *Recognitio Mortis Parentum tempore elapso.*

" On ye 20 of August, 1721, Sarah Prime, my ten-
" der & godly mother, departed this life at Milford.
  " In the same town dyed mine aged father on y^e
" 18th of Iuly, 1736. Lam. 3, 19: Remembering mine
" affliction & my misery, ye wormwood & ye gall;
" (v. 20) my soul hath them still in remembrance, & is
" humbled in me.
  " The clouds return after the rain; & I have rea-
" son with deep humiliation to say to my God, at Job,
" ch. 10, 17: Thou renewest thy witnesses against me,
" & increasest thine indignation upon me; changes
" & war are against me, For,

" On October 3$\frac{d}{}$, 1736, after a short but violent ill-
" ness, dyed at Huntington, of the throat distemper,
" my dear Sister Hannah Prime.

" Job 17 : 14 : I have said to corruption, thou art
" my father, to the worm, thou art my mother & my
" sister.

" Ebenezer Prime & Margaret Sylvester were mar-
" ried at Shelter-Island Oct. 2nd, 1723, by ye Rev. M^r
" Benjamin Woolsey, of Southold.

" Ebenezer, Son of Ebenezer Prime & Margaret
" his wife, was born at Huntington, July ye 11th, 1724,
" between one & two post meridiem, it being Satur-
" day, & baptized July ye 12th anno eodem.

" Margaret, daughter of Ebenezer Prime & Mar-
" garet his wife, was born at Huntington on Saturday
" morning about two or three of ye clock, it being
" April ye 9th, 1726. Baptized the day following.

" *Horresco Referens.*

" On the 26th day of Sept., 1726, between twelve &
" one post meridiem, Margaret, wife of Ebenezer Prime,
" ye Beloved wife of his Youth, departed this life in
" Huntington, having lived in a married state three
" years wanting six days.

" Ebenezer Prime & Experience Youngs were mar-
" ried at Southold, November ye 12th, 1730, by y^e
" Rev. Mr Benjn Woolsey, of Southold.

" Mary Prime, daughter of Ebenezer Prime & Ex-
" perience his wife, was born at Huntington, Sep^t y^e
" 12th, 1731, at about 12 o'clock in ye morning, & bap-
" tized Sept. ye 19th anno eodem.

" Sarah Prime, Daughter of Ebenezer Prime &
" Experience his wife, was born at Huntington, Sept.
" ye 15th, 1732, on Friday, about eight o'clock in y^e
" morning, & baptized ye Lord's day following, Sept.
" 17th ;
" And dyed, Precious Babe! December 12th, 1732,
" aged three months, wanting three days.
" God is righteous in all his ways & holy in all his
works. Rom. v: 13, 14.

" Benjamin Youngs Prime, son of Ebenezer Prime
" & Experience his wife, was born December ye 9th,
" 1733, at about 8 or 9 o'clock in the morning, it being
" the Lord's day, & was baptized in the afternoon
" of the same.

" Breach upon breach! Job 16: 14. On ye first
" day of January, 1733–4, dyed at Huntington, in child-
" bed, Experience Prime, the second wife of Ebenezer
" Prime, in the 35th year of her age; being born at
" Southold, Novemb^r ye 6th, 1699, & having lived in
" a married state three years, one month, & nineteen
" days. Job 10: 12.

" Gen. 11 : 28 : And Haran died before his father
" in the land of his nativity. But when the order of
" nature is inverted, the appointment of God takes
" place & is executed. Heb. ix: 27.

" Wednesday morning, Octob^r 20, 1742, between
" one & two, my dear Son Ebenezer Prime departed
" this life, aged 18 years, 3 months, & 9 days. And
" I trust is now triumphing with Christ in glory.[1] With

---

[1] Ebenezer Prime, Jr., whose death is here recorded, was a student
in Yale College. While in his junior year, and spending a vacation
at his home in Huntington, he was taken ill with a fever. He had

"low submission, O God! enable me to bow to thy
" D. sovereignty, for Jesus' sake. Amen.

" January 19th, 1749–50. Alas! Alas! I have rea-
" son to mourn bitterly & to be deeply humbled
" before the Lord; For on this day, between eleven
" & twelve, departed this life my dear daughter
" Margaret Brown, in Huntington, wife to the Rev.
" Mr. James Brown, of Bridgehampton, aged 23
" years 9 months & 10 days.

" The only branch of my family by my first mar-
" riage is now taken away. But blessed be God for
" the abundant reason I have to hope that she is now
" triumphing with Christ in glory, whither I trust her
" dear brother ascended more than three years ago.

" But, Alas! Alas! I am here in a world of sin &
" sorrow. The root is waxed old & dried up in the
" earth, & both the sprigs are cut off as with a prun-
" ing hook, so that I am as a poor old tree bereaved
" of these precious branches. Yet I desire to bless
" God & to say, as in Job 1 : 21.

given evidence of sincere piety, and had been admitted to the communion of the church. When informed that his end was near, after
addressing a few affectionate and earnest words of exhortation to
his younger brother, he exclaimed: "My flesh and my heart faileth,
but God is the strength of my heart, and my portion forever;" and
immediately passed away. Most affectionate allusions to his early
death and his lovely Christian character are made in the diaries both
of his father and his brother. The following inscription was placed
upon his tombstone: —

> " Here lies a youth, adult in virtue grown,
>   In whom the beams of heavenly knowledge shone;
>   His early zeal, the consequence of faith,
>   Denotes him bless'd in his lamented death;
>   Too good to live, he quits this earthly stage
>   T'enjoy the bliss of an eternal age."

" Ebenezer Prime & Hannah Carll were married at
" Huntington, March ye 11th, 1751/2 O. S., by ye Rev.
" Mr Naphtali Dagget.

" Dec. ye 10th, 1756. This day departed this life
" my dear & only daughter, Mary, the wife of Jer.
" Wood, aged 25 years, 2 months, & 19 days, having
" lived in a married state 3 years, 3 months, & 24
" days. Left two motherless, a son & daughter.
" A bitter day! a bitter dispensation! But Oh how
" much more bitter is Sin! my sins! Yet blessed be
" God, I do not mourn altogether without hope.

" On Fryday morning, about 6 o'clock, February y^e
" 9th, 1776, my third loving wife departed this life,
" having completed the 70th year of her age."

End of records by Ebenezer Prime.

——

Ebenezer Prime, as appears from the foregoing records,
was three times married.

First Marriage: Oct. 2, 1723, to Margaret Sylvester, of Shelter Island, by whom he had two children;
namely, —

Ebenezer, born July 11, 1724, died at Huntington,
Oct. 20, 1742;

Margaret, born April 9, 1726, married Dec. 14, 1749,
to Rev. James Brown, of Bridgehampton, died Jan. 19,
1750;

Margaret Sylvester, wife of Rev. Ebenezer Prime,
died Sept. 26, 1726.

Second Marriage: Nov. 12, 1730, to Experience
Youngs, of Southold, Long Island, who was born Nov.
6, 1699. She was a daughter of Benjamin Youngs, and

granddaughter of the Rev. John Youngs, first minister of Southold, who came from Hingham, Norfolk, England, in 1640, with his church, to New Haven, Conn., where his church was reorganized, and whence pastor and people together went to Southold. The sister of Experience Youngs was the mother of John Ledyard, the celebrated traveller, who accompanied Captain Cook on his third voyage around the world.

The children of Ebenezer and Experience Youngs Prime were:

1. Mary, born Sept. 12, 1731, who was married to Israel Wood, of Huntington, Long Island, Aug. 16, 1753, and died Dec. 10, 1756.

2. Sarah, born Sept. 15, 1732, and died December 12 the same year.

3. Benjamin Youngs, born Dec. 20, 1733, o. s. His mother, Experience Youngs Prime, died Jan. 1, 1734, leaving him an infant three weeks old.

Benjamin Youngs Prime survived all his immediate kindred. By him alone in this particular line of the family the name of PRIME was perpetuated. On coming of age he dropped the final letter of his middle name, being known thereafter as Benjamin Young Prime.

Third Marriage: March 11, 1751, o. s., to Hannah Carll, widow, who died Feb. 9, 1776.

A parchment-bound volume, now in the hands of the writer, contains a Diary by Mr. Prime, commenced when he entered upon his ministry at Huntington, and extending to the year 1764, — a period of forty-five years. It is entitled MISCELLANEA QUÆDAM, AUT EPHEMERIS

MEDITATIONUM DIVINARUM, USUI PRIVATO, E. P. DE-
LINEATA, etc. The first entry possesses historic as well
as personal interest. It is a copy of the original Church
Covenant adopted by the Milford Church on its organization at New Haven, Aug. 22, 1639 : —

" A copy of Milford Church Covenant, unto which
" I confented & into which I entred with the Lord
" & with y⁶ members of Xts Church at Milford, when
" I was made a member in full communion wᵗʰ the
" church abovefᵈ.
" Anno Domini, 1719.

" Since it hath pleased y⁶ Lord of his infinite good-
" nefs & free grace to Call us, a company of poor
" miferable wretches, out of the world unto fellowſhip
" with himfelf in Jesus X, & to bestow himfelf upon
" us by an Everlasting Covenant of his free grace,
" sealed in the blood of Jesus Christ, to be our God, &
" to make & avouch us to be his people, & hath un-
" dertaken to circumcizé our hearts, yᵗ we may love
" y⁶ Lord Our God & fear him & walk in his ways,
" wee Therefore do this day avouch y⁶ Lord to be Our
" God, Even Jehovah the only true God, the Almighty
" maker of heaven & earth, the God & father of Our
" Lord Jesus Christ; & we do this day Enter Into an
" holy Covenant with y⁶ Lord & one with another
" thro' y⁶ Grace & help of Christ Strengthening us
" (without wᵐ we can do nothing) to deny our Selves &
" all ungodliness & worldly Lusts, & all Corruptions
" & pollutions wherein in any Sort we have walked :
" & do give up ourfelves wholly to y⁶ Lord Jesus
" Christ to be taught & governed by him in all our

" Relations, Conditions, & Conversations in this world,
" avouching him to be our only prophet & teacher,
" our only prieſt & propitiation, our only king & law-
" giver: and we further bind ourſelves in his strength
" to walk before him in all proffeſsed subjection to all
" his holy ordinances according to the Rules of the
" Gospel, & alſo to walk together with this church &
" the members thereof in all brotherly love & holy
" watchfulneſs to yᵉ mutual building up one another
" in faith & Love; all which yᵉ Lord help us to per-
" form through his Rich Grace in Christ according to
" this Covenant.

" Amen.

" Subſc : by = E. Prime."

Soon after taking charge of the church at Huntington, the Rev. Ebenezer Prime purchased a farm with a
residence near the church, which remained in the possession and occupancy of himself and his direct descendants of the name more than a hundred and fifty years.
Here he devoted himself to the care of his flock,
to preparation for his pulpit services, and to general
study; enjoying the affection and commanding the respect of all whom he reached with his influence. He is
described by one of his contemporaries as " a man of
" sterling character, of powerful intellect, who possessed
" the reputation of an able and faithful divine." Culti-
vating, from the commencement of his ministry, a taste
for learning, he early began the collection of what
became, for that period, a large and valuable library,
chiefly imported from England, and including choice
editions of the Greek and Latin classics ; many of his
theological works being London editions in large folio.

A portion of his own and of his son's library which escaped the vandalism of the British soldiers in the Revolutionary War was subsequently destroyed by fire, but a few of the volumes still remain, distributed among their descendants. Of these are Pool's " Synopsis Criti-"corum," Latin, large folio ; Matthew Henry's Commentary, 6 vols. folio; Bishop Burnet's "History of the "English Reformation," 3 vols. folio; Florio's translation of Montaigne's Essays, quarto; an Aldine edition of Martial, etc.

Mr. Prime kept a register of his sermons, with the texts, dates, and places of their delivery ; from which it appears that he prepared more than three thousand. This register, and also a large number of the discourses, are still preserved. They are written in a clear hand, and give evidence of careful study and preparation. Some of his discourses on special occasions were printed and are to be found in collections of American publications of the last century. Two of these were on " The "Divine Institution of Preaching the Gospel," and on "Ordination to the Gospel Ministry." He held some peculiar views in regard to the gospel commission, maintaining that authority to preach the gospel could be conferred only by the laying on of the hands of the Presbytery, as in the case of ordination to the full work of the ministry.[1]

[1] In a note to one of his printed sermons on ordination, Mr. Prime says : —

" The Licensing of Candidates to preach without Ordination having " obtained as a custom long before I had a being, upon my entering "into the Ministry I came into & continued in it for many years, as "there was Occasion, without my particular Examination of the Point " 'Till for some Years past, my Mind being filled with Hesitations &

Mr. Prime was by birth and education a Congrega-
tionalist; and the church of which he was pastor — in
common with the other churches on the island, of Puri-
tan origin — was Independent. But early in his ministry he became convinced that the Presbyterian form of
government was better adapted for promoting order
and discipline in the church.

Several neighboring pastors who were of the same
mind resolved to hold a meeting for conference and
prayer on the subject. Accordingly, as the record states,
"A number of the ministers of the gospel within the
"County of Suffolk, on the Island of Nassau, in the Pro-
"vince of New York, convened at Southampton, April
"the 8th, 1747, in order to concert measures for the
" promotion of the great Redeemer's kingdom, especially
"within the above-mentioned bounds; and having taken
" into consideration the broken state of the churches of
"Christ within said County, the prevalence of separations
"and divisions, together with the growing mischiefs these
" disorders are big with; after repeated addresses at the
"throne of grace for divine direction," — they came to
the conclusion that the disorders spoken of were owing to
"the want of stated rules of ecclesiastical government."
Accordingly, they voted to organize themselves into a
Presbytery, to be called "the Presbytery of Suffolk,"
and adopted the Westminster Confession of Faith, Cate-

"Doubts put me upon a more critical Inquiry into the Orders of
"Christ's House; & finding that as all ministerial Power is derived
"from Christ to the ordinary Ministers of the Gospel, by the grand
"Commission, Mat. XXVIII., & that they, according to divine Institu-
"tion, are invested with those Powers by Ordination, so Preaching the
"Gospel being one principal Branch of their Work, none consequent-
"ly have a right to preach the Gospel but those that are ordain'd."

chisms, Directory for Worship and Discipline. The
Rev. Ebenezer Prime was chosen the first moderator,
and, with the Rev. Samuel Buel, of Easthampton, was
appointed to attend the Synod of New York to request
that the Presbytery might be received into that body.
The request was granted, and the Congregational
churches on Long Island generally became connected
with the Presbytery. Almost from the time of their
organization these churches, together with many of
those of the same order in Connecticut, were quite
commonly called Presbyterian.[1]

In the early part of the French and Indian War
(1756–63), which ended with the conquest of Canada

---

[1] The following Declaration was made, in 1799, by the Hartford
North Association of Ministers, composed of such men as Drs. Strong
and Flint of Hartford, and Dr. Perkins of West Hartford :—

"This Association gives information to all whom it may concern,
"that the constitution of the churches in the State of Connecticut,
"founded on the common usages and the Confession of Faith, Heads
"of Agreement, and Articles of Church Discipline, adopted at the
"earliest period of the settlement of the State, is not Congregational,
"but contains the essentials of the government of the Church of Scot-
"land, or [the] Presbyterian Church in America, particularly as it gives
"a decisive power to ecclesiastical councils ; and a Consociation, con-
"sisting of ministers and messengers, or a lay representation from the
"churches, is possessed of substantially the same authority as Presby-
"tery. The churches, therefore, in Connecticut at large, and in our
"district in particular, are not now, and never were, from the earliest
"period of our settlement, Congregational Churches, according to the
"ideas and forms of church order contained in the Book of Discipline
"called the Cambridge Platform. There are, however, scattered over
"the State, perhaps ten or twelve churches (unconsociated) which are
"properly called Congregational, agreeably to the rules of church
"discipline in the book above mentioned. Sometimes, indeed, the As-
"sociated Churches of Connecticut are loosely and vaguely, though
"improperly, termed Congregational." (See Gillett's "History of
the Presbyterian Church," i. 438, 439.)

by the English, a regiment of Provincials was raised in Suffolk County to join the expedition against Quebec. They assembled at Huntington, May 7, 1759, and Mr. Prime was invited to preach to them, which he did from the text, Judges iv. 14: "And Deborah said unto "Barak, Up; for this is the day in which the Lord hath "delivered Sisera into thine hand: is not the Lord gone "out before thee?" The discourse was printed, in compliance with the request of the "Soldiers, Inhabitants, "and Strangers that were hearers." A printed copy, and also the original manuscript, are preserved among the family papers.

The long-extended ministry of Mr. Prime at Huntington was greatly blessed in promoting the spiritual welfare of the people, and at different periods in large additions to the church. In common with many others on the Island, this congregation was specially visited in "The Great Awakening" of 1740–41. In his private diary Mr. Prime makes repeated mention of the scenes that accompanied this remarkable religious movement. As showing the prevailing influence, he mentions that on one occasion, when the people were gathered together at a "military training" (usually a scene of a very different character), he was requested to preach to the assembled multitude, and adds: "At this meeting the main "part of the congregation were in tears, and several were "brought under strong convictions." A few days later he writes: "Preached on John vii. 37. Great numbers "cried out in distress; the power of God was marvel-"lous." At a much later period (Sept. 2, 1764), when he was assisted at a communion season by his friend, the Rev. Dr. Buel, of Easthampton, he writes: "God "has poured out his Spirit in a surprising manner "upon this people. Glory be to his name!"

In the War of the Revolution, immediately after the battle of Long Island, which was fought Aug. 27, 1776, the British took possession of the whole Island and held it until the conclusion of the war. It was extensively ravaged again and again, and those who favored the cause of the Colonies were made the victims of British and Tory vengeance. The property of the inhabitants was rudely confiscated or wantonly destroyed. Those who had been at all conspicuous by their patriotism were compelled to flee to the mainland, or were treated with personal severity. The churches and congregations were in many cases broken up, and for seven years an almost chaotic state of things existed.

There was one conspicuous example of a pastor who was allowed to minister to those of his flock who remained in their homes and on their farms. The Rev. Samuel Buel, D.D., who has just been mentioned, was the third pastor in succession at Easthampton whose ministry in that church extended over half a century. He was a man of learning, of eloquence, and of unbounded influence with his people. The veneration in which he was held was so proverbial that a British officer stationed at the place once asked to be permitted to see Dr. Buel. When he left his presence he remarked, "I have seen the god of Easthampton." Dr. Buel was warmly attached to the cause of the Colonies, and did not conceal his sentiments; but he decided to stay with his people and share with them the fortunes of the war. Such, however, was the respect that his character inspired among the officers of the British army, he was

allowed to remain unmolested during the whole of the
conflict without in any measure compromising his patriotism ; and he was often able by his influence to obtain
a mitigation of the treatment of his parishioners and
others who favored the American cause.[1]

No part of Long Island suffered more severely in the
war than Huntington, the parish of Mr. Prime, which
was a prosperous town, and specially important to the
enemy on account of its central position and its well-

---

[1] Dr. Buel's gentlemanly bearing and sparkling wit made him a
special favorite with Sir William Erskine, who was commander of the
British forces in that part of the Island, and the traditions of Easthampton have many anecdotes of their intercourse. At one time Sir
William informed Dr. Buel that he had issued an order to the people
of his parish to appear with their teams and tools at Southampton the
next day (which was the Sabbath), to attend to some work which he
wished done at that time. Dr. Buel replied that he had heard of the
order, but being commander-in-chief on that day, he had countermanded
it. The precedence of the pastor on the Lord's day was pleasantly
admitted, and the order was revoked.

On another occasion Dr. Buel was invited by Sir William Erskine
to join a party of British officers in a deer-hunt. Being behind the
appointed hour in making his appearance on the ground, the entire
party, tired of waiting, had mounted when he arrived. The younger
officers (of whom Lord Percy, afterward Duke of Northumberland,
was one) manifested no little impatience at the delay, especially as it
was caused by a rebel parson. Their chagrin was increased by an
order from Sir William to dismount to receive his friend with becoming respect. Lord Percy, being introduced, did not conceal his ill-
humor, and on being asked by Dr. Buel what portion of his Majesty's
forces he had the honor to command, replied, with an evident intent to
insult the clergyman, "A legion of devils just from hell." "Then,"
said Dr. Buel, "I suppose I have the honor to address Beelzebub, the
prince of the devils." Lord Percy, stung by the witty repartee, in-
stantly put his hand to his sword, but was rebuked by Sir William;
and though the laugh of the party was turned upon Percy, the polite-
ness and pleasantry of Dr. Buel restored his good-humor before the
day was over, and compelled him to respect and admire the man whom
in his resentment he had called "an old rebel."

protected harbor. The British troops were quartered on the inhabitants, whom they treated with all the rigors of war, destroying their crops and wasting their goods, or using them without recompense. The Presbyterian church, in which Mr. Prime had so long ministered, was taken for a military depot, and the pulpit and pews were broken up and used for fuel. The pastor's house was occupied by the troops, and his valuable library used for lighting fires, mutilated by the destruction of portions of sets of books, or recklessly scattered abroad. His study-chair, which still remains in the family, bears the marks of the rough usage to which all his property was subjected. He was an object of special hostility on account of his having warmly espoused and advocated the cause of the country before the war broke out. Driven from his own home in his seventy-seventh year, he retired to a quiet part of the parish, preaching in private houses wherever he could gather any of his people together. He died before the war was over, having ministered to this one church for sixty years. He was buried among his people in the ancient cemetery, and a stone was erected at the head of his grave with this inscription : —

In Memory of

The REV^D EBENEZER PRIME,

Ob. Sept. 25, 1779,

Æ 79.

This head-stone, with others marking the graves of members of his family who had died previous to the war, has a curious history in connection with those troublous times. The cemetery covered a hill in the midst of the village of Huntington, overlooking the town and harbor. Toward the close of the war Colonel Thompson, of the British army (afterward Count Rumford), was sent with a body of troops to occupy the place. By his orders the venerable church building in which Mr. Prime had so long ministered was torn down, and the timber used for constructing barracks and blockhouses in the cemetery, which was occupied as a fort.[1] The graves were levelled, and the gravestones used by the soldiers for the bottoms of their ovens. The traditions of Huntington state that the loaves of bread came out of the ovens bearing, in relief and in reverse, the inscription, "IN MEMORY OF," etc. Colonel Thompson, who was violent in his hostility to the American cause, and who cherished a special hatred to the memory of the late patriotic pastor, had the grave of Mr. Prime pointed out, and gave orders that his own marquee should be pitched at the head of it, so that he might have the satisfaction of treading on the "—— old rebel" every time he went in and out of his tent.

Several years after the war was over, on the first occurrence of a death in the family, the friends went into the graveyard to select a place for the burial as near as possible to the former location of the family graves, then completely obliterated. One of the per-

---

[1] By a noteworthy coincidence, this ancient church was wantonly demolished on the very day on which the Preliminary Treaty of Peace was signed by the Commissioners of Great Britain and the United States, at Paris, Nov. 30, 1782. It was a fitting close to the numerous acts of vandalism perpetrated by the British soldiery on Long Island during the war.

sons, having an iron bar in his hand, let it drop with the point upon the ground, saying, "I think it was just about here." The iron, sinking into the soil, struck something that sounded hollow, and on removing the earth the old pastor's head-stone was discovered. On further examination they found the head-stones of all the members of the family who had died before and during the early years of the war. They had been taken up by some careful hand, laid upon the graves a few inches below the surface, and covered with earth. The explanation was, that when the pastor's family were driven from their home by the British, the house and farm were left in charge of an old colored servant, a slave, who died during the war. It was presumed that when he saw the graveyard about to be occupied as a fort by the British troops, the graves levelled, and the head-stones destroyed, he took up the family stones and laid them flat upon the graves to which they severally belonged, covering them with earth sufficiently to protect them from observation and disturbance. These stones, replaced, are now standing (1888), the only monuments in this ancient cemetery which antedate the Revolutionary War.

The following is a list of the publications of the Rev. Ebenezer Prime, copies of all which are still preserved in the family : —

PUBLICATIONS OF THE REV. EBENEZER PRIME, A.M.

THE PASTOR AT LARGE VINDICATED, From a Consideration of the Edification of Christ's Mystical Body as the great End & Design of the Institution & Perpetuation of the Evangelical Ministry; in a SERMON Preached at the Oyster Ponds, on Long Island, Nov. 10, 1757, Previous to the Ordination of the Reverend Messieurs Jonathan Barber & John Darbie. By Ebenezer Prime, A.M. & Pastor of the Presbyterian Church in Huntington, on Long Island. Published at the Desire of the Ministers Present & others. New-York: Printed & Sold by H. Gaine, at the Bible & Crown, on Hanover Square. M,DCCLVIII.

THE DIVINE INSTITUTION OF PREACHING THE GOSPEL CONSIDERED; The Nature & Quality of the Gospel Mission Opened & Illustrated, and the Necessity of an Investiture with Office Power, by Ordination, in order to the Preaching of the Gospel according to Divine Institution, evidenced & improved, in A SERMON Preached at Brook-Haven, on Long-Island, June 15, 1758, Previous to the Ordination of the Rev. Mr. Abner Brush. By Ebenezer Prime, A.M. and Pastor of the Presbyterian Church in Huntington on Long-Island. Published in Compliance with the Desire of Suffolk Presbytery. New-York: Printed & Sold by H. Gaine, at the Bible & Crown, on Hanover Square. 1758.

THE IMPORTANCE OF THE DIVINE PRESENCE WITH THE ARMIES OF GOD'S PEOPLE IN THEIR MARTIAL ENTERPRISES Considered & Improved, and a Christian Soldier Admonished, Counselled & Encouraged: a Sermon Preached to the Provincials of the County of Suffolk, at Huntington on Long Island, May 7, 1759. By Ebenezer Prime, A.M., Pastor of the Presbyterian Church in Huntington. Published in Compliance with the desires of a number of the Soldiers, Inhabitants & Strangers that were hearers. New York: Printed by Samuel Barker at the New Printing Office in Beaver Street. MD.CC.LIX.

BENJAMIN YOUNG PRIME, M.D.

BENJAMIN YOUNG PRIME, son of the Rev. Ebenezer Prime and Experience Youngs, his wife, was
born at Huntington, Long Island, Dec. 20, 1733, N. S.
His mother lived but three weeks after his birth, and
being the only surviving child, he was the object of
special solicitude and care in his training and education.
His father early instilled into his mind his own thirst
for knowledge, and thus laid the foundation for his
great attainments in classical, scientific, and professional
learning. He entered the College of New Jersey, then
located at Newark, under the presidency of the Rev.
Aaron Burr. He was graduated in 1751, sharing the
honors of the class with his intimate friend Nathaniel
Scudder.[1]

He prosecuted his medical studies under Dr. Jacob
Ogden, of Jamaica, Long Island, and commenced prac-

[1] Nathaniel Scudder was his early schoolmate, his college class-
mate and room-mate, and his fellow-student in medicine. He filled
several important offices in State; he was one of the Council of
Safety of the State of New Jersey at the opening of the Revolutionary conflict, and a member of the Continental Congress from
1777 to 1779. He was killed at Shrewsbury, N. J., Oct. 16, 1781, in
a skirmish with an invading party of British. Dr. B. Y. Prime wrote
an elegiac ode on the occasion of his death, which was published in
"MUSCIPULA," and named his youngest son Nathaniel Scudder, in
memory of his friend.

tice at Easthampton, Long Island. In 1756 he was chosen tutor in the College of New Jersey, which was removed to Princeton the same year. He accepted the appointment after much deliberation, and while fulfilling the duties of his position devoted his leisure to general literary pursuits. In 1757 he resigned the office of tutor, receiving from the Board of Trustees the following expression of their regard and appreciation of his services. This certificate is subscribed by one of the signers of the Declaration of Independence, who was then clerk of the Board of Trustees of Princeton College : —

"Thursday, the 29th of Sept., 1757.

"Mr. Prime, one of the Tutors, applying to this Board "for a dismission from his office, It is ordered that at the "request of the s^d Mr. Prime he be dismissed accord- "ingly. Nevertheless the Trustees, being fully sensible "of the abilities of the said Mr. Prime & of his having "faithfully executed his s^d office during the time of his "continuance therein, do with reluctance part with the "s^d Mr. Prime; & as a testimony of their sense of his "good conduct & merit, do present him with £10 over "& above his salary, & are sorry that the smallness of "their fund will not admit of their giving him a larger "sum.

"Signed,   RICHARD STOCKTON, Clk."

In 1760 he received the honorary degree of A.M. from Yale College, having taken the same, in course, at Princeton College.

After a few years' practice Dr. Prime resolved to visit some of the medical schools of Europe, in order to enjoy better advantages for perfecting his knowledge and experience in medicine and surgery than this country at that time afforded. He had already become an accomplished general scholar, and had made himself master of several languages. Under the instruction of his father he had become familiar with the Hebrew; he not only read the ancient Greek and Latin authors as freely as English poetry or history, but his published works contain poems in both these languages. At one period of his life it was his favorite pastime to write in Latin verse, and he left among his papers Latin versifications of one of the Psalms in all the varieties of metre of the Odes of Horace. Among his published writings is an extended Greek poem. He had also acquired several modern languages, in which he wrote and spoke with as much facility as in his own. He was accordingly well prepared to profit by a visit to the European universities and capitals.

He embarked at New York for England, June 16, 1762. The vessel was attacked on the way by a French privateer, and in the engagement Dr. Prime was wounded. He spent some months in London, where he attended a course of anatomical lectures, and enjoyed the privileges of the hospitals. He visited Edinburgh with the same objects in view, and prosecuted his studies more at length at the University of Leyden, which was once the most renowned of the universities of Europe. At that time it was the resort of scholars from England and all parts of the Continent. After a thorough medical course at this centre of learning, and after an examination (as his diploma reads) "per Universam Medicinam," on presenting a Latin

essay upon an assigned thesis, and defending the same
"prompte adversus Professorum opponentium argu-
"menta, objectionesque," he received his medical degree
at the university, July 7, 1764. His essay was published at Leyden in large quarto, and, in addition to its
scientific and literary merit, is, in typography and style
of publication, not unworthy of the celebrated seat of
learning at which it was presented and printed.

He travelled as far as Moscow, and returned to New
York, Nov. 14, 1764.[1] Of this visit to Europe the Hon.
Benjamin Thompson, the historian of Long Island, says:
" He was honored with a degree at most of the institu-
"tions, and was much noticed for his many accomplish-
"ments." While on his way homeward he published
in London a volume entitled, " THE PATRIOT MUSE; or,
"Poems on some of the Principal Events of the Late
"War in America" (the French and English).

In December, 1764, Dr. Prime commenced the practice of surgery in the city of New York. He had

[1] The Rev. Ebenezer Prime in his private diary alludes as follows
to the departure and the safe return of his son : —

"HUNTINGTON, June 14, 1762. — This day my only son & only
"child yet living took his leave of us & went to N. York, with a
"design to embark on board the Hariot packet for England. A try-
"ing season! I desire to resign him up unto the Lord, to whom I
"have given him. O may the divine presence go along with him.
"God the Father, Son, & Holy Ghost be his Father & friend, his por-
"tion, shield, & exceeding great Reward. Amen and Amen."

"NOVEMBER 17, 1764. — Last Tuesday my son, my only son & only
"surviving child, B. Y. P., returned from Europe to N. York, & this
" day came to us in Huntington, having been gone from us two Years,
"five Months, & three Days. Glory be to God for his great Good-
"ness, in numerous instances of it, to him, & to us, abroad & at
"home, & for his safe return. All our salvations are of God. To
" Him be all the Glory, for ever & ever. Amen.

"E. P."

scarcely entered upon his professional career when the wrongs of the American Colonies at the hands of the English Government began to awaken public discussion. With the enthusiasm of a true patriot, he threw himself into the conflict, foreseeing that it was to be a struggle for liberty, if not for independence. He had been loyal to the mother-country in her contest with the French for supremacy in America, but he was still more ardent in defending the Colonies against the oppressive measures adopted by the British Government in its endeavor to hold them in absolute subjection. The time had not yet come for drawing the sword, but he took up the pen and wielded it with effect. On the passage of the Stamp Act he wrote "A Song for the Sons of Liberty in New York," which was extensively used to stir up the spirit of American patriotism. The following stanzas are taken from one of the printed copies : —

> " In story we 're told
> How our fathers of old
> Braved the rage of the winds and the waves,
> And crossed the deep o'er
> To this desolate shore,
> All because they were loath to be slaves, Brave boys,
> All because they were loath to be slaves.

> " Heav'n only controls
> The great deep as it rolls ;
> And the tide which our continent laves
> Emphatical roars
> This advice to our shores,
> O Americans, never be slaves, Brave boys !
> O Americans, never be slaves.

" The birthright we hold
    Shall never be sold,
But sacred maintain'd to our graves ;
    And before we 'll comply
    We will gallantly die,
For we must not, we will not, be slaves, Brave boys ;
For we must not, we will not be slaves ! "

When the Rev. Ebenezer Prime was becoming en-feebled by age, Dr. B. Y. Prime, being his only surviving child, gave up his lucrative practice in the city and took up his residence at Huntington, to watch over his father's declining years. They dwelt together in the old homestead, and while discharging the duties of their respective professions, spent much time in their favorite literary and scientific pursuits. The son had provided himself with chemical and philosophical apparatus, and was much interested in electrical experiments, having been moved thereto by the discussions which followed the discoveries of Dr. Benjamin Franklin. He was an astronomer as well as a mathematician. Among the numerous and varied scientific papers which he left behind him are elaborate calculations of the orbits of the planets and the erratic movements of comets. Devoted with equal ardor to the cause of the country, the condition of which was constantly assuming graver importance, both father and son labored earnestly to fan the flame of patriotism which was burning in the hearts of the people, and to prepare the way for coming independence.

Soon after he had settled himself at Huntington, Dr. Prime received a visit from his kinsman, the renowned but eccentric traveller, John Ledyard, whose name has been mentioned in the family genealogy. Ledyard began his wanderings over a great part of the known world by abruptly leaving Dartmouth College in 1773 and spending several months among the Indians of the " Six Nations." Returning through Canada to the headwaters of the Connecticut, he dug out with his own hands from a log, after the style of the Indians, a canoe, in which, with a Bible and a copy of Ovid for his only companions, he floated down the river. Crossing the Sound, he made a tour of Long Island on horseback. In a characteristic letter written to his friends soon after, among other incidents of the journey he made mention of his visit to the home at Huntington : —

" At Easthampton I met with a kind reception from " the Rev. Mr. Buel, moderator of the Synod, an influ- " ential man and a glorious preacher. . . . After a ride of " about one hundred miles I arrived at Huntington, a " large town about forty miles from New York, where " I visited the minister of the place, old Mr. Prime. " After about twelve days' feasting upon his great " library, and a quickly made friendship with Dr. " (B. Y.) Prime, formerly of New York, I returned to " Mr. Buel's, and stayed a short time with that her- " mit, where and with whom I longed to be buried in " ease."

On the 18th of December, 1774, Dr. Prime married Mary Wheelwright, widow of the Rev. John Greaton, rector of the Episcopal Church at Huntington. She was born at Boston, July 10, 1744, and was the great-great-granddaughter of the Rev. John Wheelwright, founder and pastor of Exeter, N. H. Her maternal grandfather, Colonel Goffe, commanded a regiment of Provincials in the expedition against Louisburg in 1745, when this fortress was captured from the French by New England troops, some of whom lived to take part in the battle of Bunker Hill, thirty years later.

At the opening of the Revolutionary War, when Long Island fell into the hands of the British, Dr. Benjamin Y. Prime was compelled to flee from the island to escape the vengeance of the enemy, which he had aroused by his patriotic writings. With his wife and child he crossed into Connecticut, where he remained until the conclusion of peace in 1783,—a period of seven years. He resided at New Haven and Wethersfield, three of his children being born during this exile. The departure of the family was so sudden that they were compelled to abandon the homestead with all its contents, furniture, library and valuables, to the ravages of the soldiery. Mrs. Prime hastily put the family silver into a canvas sack and secretly dropped it into a well, where it remained during the seven years of the war, in which the well was in constant use, no one suspecting the treasure it contained. When the war was over and the family returned to their home, reinforced by three children who had been born in Connecticut in the mean time, the sack with its contents was drawn up, not a piece of silver missing or injured. These relics, including tankards and goblets, are still preserved in various branches of the family as heirlooms and memorials of the experiences of the Revolutionary period.[1]

[1] These pieces of silver are engraved with the arms of the Wheelwright family, which Mary Wheelwright bore as heiress of the estate. She inherited large tracts of land in New Hampshire and Maine, of

In mature life Dr. Prime became a man of humble
piety, and illustrated in his personal walk and professional career the influence of the early instructions,
the life-long counsels, and the consistent example of
his godly father. An autobiographical sketch, without
date, entitled "Some Remarkable Passages in the Life
"of B. Y. P.," is a record of several striking providences
in the early years of the writer which had made a deep
impression upon him. A diary, running through a
series of years, found after his death among his private
papers, contains an almost daily record of his spiritual
exercises, with frequent references to the emotions
awakened by his visits to his patients. Among his
published poems is one entitled, "Meditation over a
"Dying Patient," commencing, —

"Well! I have done : I can no more,
  But must my baffled aim deplore ;
  I 'll lay my drugs and cordials by,
  For art is vain, and he must die."

Dr. B. Y. Prime died suddenly of apoplexy at Huntington, Oct. 31, 1791. His widow, Mary Wheelwright
Prime, lived to an advanced age. She was a woman of
remarkable vigor of intellect and great practical wisdom.
Left by the death of her husband with five young
children, with a farm and a large property which had

which portions were sold from time to time down to 1798. In the
year 1826 she made a deed of gift of all her then unsold lands to her
son, Nathaniel S. Prime. Although situated in New England, they
were esteemed wild lands, for which there was no sale ; and when in
later times they had become valuable, Mr. Prime declined to assert
his title as against actual settlers or holders in good faith, and they
were suffered to pass out of the family.

become depreciated in value by the ravages of war, and involved by expenses incurred during the seven years' exile of the family, she managed the estate with such prudence and sagacity that it was wholly redeemed from embarrassment. She brought up her children with exemplary fidelity and success, and gave to each of them a good education. Possessed of a strong constitution, she survived and recovered from repeated attacks of paralysis, retaining her mental vigor to the last. She died March 7, 1835, aged 90 years and 8 months. Her epitaph, written by herself, was in these words :—

HER FRAILTIES AND INFIRMITIES BURY WITH HER :

IF THERE WAS ANYTHING COMMENDABLE IN HER LIFE,

PRACTISE AND FOLLOW IT.

The children of Benjamin Young Prime and Mary Wheelwright his wife were : —

1. Ebenezer, born at Huntington, Long Island, Oct. 7, 1775 ; died at Huntington, Feb. 20, 1842 ;

2. Liberty, born at Wethersfield, Conn., Oct. 13, 1777 ; died at New York, May 20, 1855 ;

3. Ann Wheelwright, born at New Haven, Conn., Jan. 10, 1780 ; died at Huntington, Sept. 18, 1813 ;

4. Mary Wood, born at New Haven, Conn., Sept. 1, 1782 ; died at New York, Feb. 25, 1835 ;

5. NATHANIEL SCUDDER, born at Huntington, Long Island, April 21, 1785 ; died at Mamaroneck, N. Y., March 27, 1856.

PUBLICATIONS OF BENJAMIN Y. PRIME, M.D.

DISSERTATIO MEDICA INAUGURALIS, De Fluxu Muliebri
Menstruo, Quam, Favente Summo Numine, Ex Auctoritate
Magnifici Rectoris, Ewaldi Hollebeek, Theologiæ Doctoris
et Professoris in Acad. Lugd. Bat. Ordinarii, nec non
Amplissimi Senatus Academici Consensu, et Nobilissimæ
Facultatis Medicæ Decreto, Pro Gradu Doctoratus, Sum-
misque in Medicina Honoribus et Privilegiis, ritè ac
legitimè consequendis, Eruditorum Examini fubmittit.
Benjaminus Young Prime, A. M.   Nov.-Eboracensis
Americanus.   Ad diem 7 Julii MDCCLXIV. H. L. Q. S.
Lugduni Batavorum, Apud Theodorum Haak, 1764.
pp. 46.

THE PATRIOT MUSE; or, Poems on some of the Principal Events of the Late War : Together with a Poem on
the Peace : Vincit Amor Patriæ. By an American Gentleman. London. 1764. 8vo. pp. 94.

COLUMBIA'S GLORY; or, British Pride Humbled: A
Poem on the American Revolution : Some part of it being a Parody on an Ode entitled Britain's Glory; or, Gal-
lic Pride Humbled : composed on the Capture of Quebec,
A. D. 1759. By Benjamin Young Prime, M. D. New
York: Printed by Thomas Greenleaf for the Author.
1791.

MUSCIPULA: Sive Cambromyomachia.   The Mouse-
trap; or, the Battle of the Welsh and the Mice : in Latin
and English.   With Other Poems in different Languages.
By an American.   New York: M. W. Dodd.   pp. 96.
1840.   [The English translation of the Muscipula is the
work of Dr. B. Y. P. ; the other poems are original.]

REV. NATHANIEL S. PRIME, D.D.

NATHANIEL SCUDDER PRIME, son of Benjamin Young Prime, M.D., and Mary Wheelwright, his wife, was born at Huntington, Long Island, April 21, 1785. He was baptized, was admitted to the communion of the church, was licensed to preach the gospel, preached his first sermon, was ordained to the ministry, and at length preached his semi-centennial sermon, all in the same church edifice, which was erected the year before his birth on the spot where the church building occupied by his grandfather during the whole sixty years of his ministry had been torn down by the British just at the close of the Revolutionary War. His father dying when the son was only six years old, his mother had the care of his education. He pursued his preparatory studies at Huntington Academy, and entered the College of New Jersey (at Princeton), under the presidency of the Rev. Dr. Samuel Stanhope Smith. Among the active professors of the College at that time was one for whom Mr. Prime always expressed the warmest regard, — John Maclean, M.D., father of the Rev. Dr. John Maclean, late President of the College.

While Mr. Prime was in his Sophomore year, the college building, Nassau Hall, which had been erected before the Revolution, and which was then "the largest "stone edifice in America," was set on fire at noonday, March 2, 1802, and was consumed, with the exception of the substantial walls, which have withstood two conflagrations.[1] This venerable structure, the interior having been twice restored, is now standing, the central figure of one of the finest ranges of college buildings grouped together in the world, — certainly unsurpassed in this country. The writer has heard his father narrate some very amusing incidents connected with the fire of 1802, by which the whole body of the students were driven out to seek quarters in the town and the surrounding country. Mr. Prime was graduated in 1804, in the largest class which up to that time ever left the institution. Among his classmates were the Hon. Theodore Frelinghuysen, Hon. Joseph R. Ingersoll, Rev. Philip Lindsley, D.D., Hon. Samuel L. Southard, etc.

When he left college there was no well-established theological seminary in the country to which he could resort in preparation for his chosen life-work, the gospel ministry. Accordingly, he pursued his studies at Huntington, in the mode common at that day, under the counsel of his pastor, the Rev. William Schenck, and with the advice of other neighboring ministers, entering at once upon such practical service as every congregation afforded, — a kind of theological training-school which has sent out into the great field a host of laborers who would compare most favorably, in fitness and ministerial success, with the graduates of the theological seminaries of the present day.

[1] Nassau Hall was burned the second time March 10, 1855.

Among those to whom Mr. Prime was largely indebted for counsel, both before and after entering the ministry, were the Rev. Dr. Aaron Woolworth, of Bridgehampton, one of the most saintly ministers of his day; the Rev. Herman Dagget, of Fireplace, a man of great dignity, who, according to all local report, "was never known to laugh," but who was proverbially genial in character and manners, and of whom the remark was made by one of his co-presbyters, "Brother "Dagget is just fit to preach to ministers;" and the Rev. Lyman Beecher, then settled at Easthampton, to whom Mr. Prime was wont to acknowledge himself as greatly indebted for fraternal advice during the first years of his ministry, while he was settled at Sag Harbor, a few miles distant from Easthampton.

He was licensed by the Presbytery of Long Island, Oct. 10, 1805, at Huntington, where he preached his first sermon among his kindred and friends. He immediately left home on a missionary tour eastward on the Island. Stopping, an entire stranger, at Cutchogue, he was asked to tarry and preach on the coming Sabbath to a congregation which, owing to dissensions, had long been without a pastor. He remained at this place five months, preaching and laboring with all the ardor of a youth just entering upon the great work of his life. He succeeded in reconciling the differences among the people and in building up the church, — though not, apparently, in developing their liberality; for at the end of this term of service he received his salary at the rate of three dollars per week, and left.

He performed missionary service for several months at other places on the Island, and in the following June started to make a tour of New England on horseback. Crossing the Sound, he spent the first Sabbath at Norwalk, Conn., where he preached for the Rev. Dr. Burnett, pastor of the Congregational church. As he was taking leave of his host on Monday morning, Dr. Burnett, apparently in perfect health, accompanied him to the door, and bidding him farewell, re-entered the house. He was immediately stricken with apoplexy, and died within two hours after parting with his guest, who was then prosecuting his journey wholly ignorant of what had befallen his friend. At Meriden, Conn., Mr. Prime was seized with a severe illness, which compelled him to turn his steps homeward as soon as he was able to travel ; and it was several months before he had fully recovered from the attack.

In the autumn of 1806 he was appointed by his Presbytery to supply the pulpit of the church at Sag Harbor. His labors here were marked by an extensive religious awakening, in which, within the space of six months, one hundred persons in the congregation became hopefully the subjects of renewing grace, and many were also added to the neighboring churches. Nearly forty years afterward, in 1845, the pastor of this church, in which Mr. Prime's ministrations had been so signally blessed, bore this testimony to their permanent results : " The stamina of this church at " this time; the piety and wisdom of the eldership ; " the ability and efficiency of Sabbath-school instruction ; " and, in a word, its power of doing good, are obviously " to be traced to the revival of 1808–9."

On the 5th of July, 1808, he married Julia Ann Jermain, daughter of Major John Jermain, of Sag

Harbor, who was the happy and useful companion of his subsequent life.[1]

He was ordained at Huntington, Oct. 24, 1809; and after preaching two years at Smithtown and Freshpond, Long Island, he left the Island for the interior of the State, spending the first winter at Milton, Saratoga County. He made the voyage up the Hudson, with his wife and two children, in a sloop, and in the ordinary length of time, seven days, — longer than is now required to cross the Atlantic.[2]

[1] The mother of Mrs. Prime, Margaret Pierson Jermain, was a lineal descendant, in the sixth generation, of Henry Pierson, who came from England to Southampton, Long Island, in 1640. John Jermain and Margaret Pierson, his wife, had four sons and five daughters, of whom all but one were born in the last century, and of whom all but two lived to be over eighty years of age ; one dying in his ninety-fifth year. One still survives, in her eighty-fourth year. They all early in life became members of the Christian Church, and have lived consistent Christian lives. They were : —

Mary, born May 7, 1782, wife of Daniel Latham; died Jan. 28, 1811, aged 29.

Sylvanus Pierson, born July 31, 1784; died April 20, 1869, aged 85.

Rebekah, born Oct. 2, 1787, wife of Alden Spooner; died Nov. 15, 1824, aged 37.

Julia Ann, born Jan. 31, 1789, wife of Rev. Nathaniel S. Prime ; died Aug. 24, 1874, aged 85.

Alanson, born Feb. 10, 1791 ; died Nov. 5, 1885, aged 94.

Caroline, born Jan. 25, 1794; wife of Rev. Stephen Porter; died June 18, 1877, aged 83.

John, born March 22, 1796 ; died March 14, 1881, aged 85.

George Washington, born Sept. 29, 1798; died Sept. 21, 1879, aged 81.

Margaret Pierson, born March 4, 1804; wife of Joseph Slocum, now living in her eighty-fourth year.

[2] To give an idea of the voyage up and down the Hudson in a sloop — the packet-ship of that day — we make an extract from the Journal of an older sister of Mr. Prime, written several years previous, in going from New York to Albany and returning. This was ten

The following summer he accepted a call to the first Presbyterian Church of Cambridge, Washington County,

years before the first steamboat passed up the Hudson. The writer of this Journal was then a girl of seventeen : —

"*April* 9, 1797. Two o'clock in the afternoon set sail from New " York for Albany ; sailed twenty miles, and dropped anchor for " that day.

" 10*th*. Head-wind continued; lay at anchor under the Palisade " mountains ; P. and myself very sick; set sail about noon; reached " West Point, and anchored for that night.

" 11*th*. Set sail in the morning; about noon reached Newburg; "landed Mr. C., Captain O. and son ; took on board Mr. W.; set sail " and came as far as Poughkeepsie ; anchored and lay all night.

" 12*th*. Set sail; came as far as Rhinebeck ; dropped anchor in "the afternoon, and went ashore.

" 13*th*. Set sail in the morning ; raining very hard ; disagreeable " sailing; toward noon began to snow ; very cold; reached Livingston " Manor. Anchored, and lay all night rolling and tossing ; very much " frightened; called to Captain Williams. After being assured there " was no danger, went to sleep, and slept till morning.

" 14*th*. In the afternoon set sail ; got as far as Catskill; cleared " off very pleasant; dropped anchor ; boatmen went on shore ; very " calm all night.

" 15*th*. Set sail, with head-wind continuing ; had a fine view of " Hudson; went to Loonenburgh ; dropped anchor, with prospect of " a storm.

" 16*th*. Lay all day at Loonenburgh ; about noon Mr. B. came " on board and invited us on shore; came on board in the evening.

" 17*th*. Wind springing up southerly, set sail in the afternoon ; "had a fine breeze ; arrived at Albany at night after a long and " tedious voyage of nine days from New York."

The return voyage was shorter by two days.

" *May* 1*st*. Set sail for New York about twelve o'clock with a fair " wind ; reached New Baltimore, where we stopped to take in wood; "raining very hard ; not able to do anything.

" 2*d*. Rainy all day ; still forced to lie idle, with a fair wind.

" 3*d*. Cleared off pleasant; wind springing up southerly, felt " quite discouraged; went on shore and gathered flowers.

" 4*th*. About eleven o'clock set sail with a head-wind ; reached " Loonenburgh about noon, with hardly perceiving that we moved at " all ; got as far as East Camp; anchored, and lay all night.

" 5*th*. Set sail in the forenoon ; wind springing up ahead ; had a

N. Y., and was installed pastor July 14, 1813. This was the scene of his longest and most important pastoral labors, and here he exerted, in other public relations, his most widely extended influence. " The Old "White Meeting-House," a volume by his son, S. Irenæus Prime, published without names of persons or place, is a faithful sketch of this pastor and his flock. The Synod of Albany, which then covered the whole northern and a large portion of the middle and western parts of the State, was more or less the field of his ecclesiastical influence.

Within less than a year after entering upon his pastorate at Cambridge, Mr. Prime performed an act which is best related in the words of his semi-centennial sermon : —

" Being now settled on a competent salary and with "a large charge, extending over twelve miles square, I "felt the importance of setting myself down to study. "And yet, from the strong desire of the congregation to

"rough time ; got as far as Rhinebeck ; went up to the dock ; Cousin "P. and myself so sick, could not help ourselves ; with the help of " Captain Schenck made out to get on shore ; felt much better. Went "up to the 'Cottage of Content,' where the brown loaf and maple ."sugar were administered with a hearty welcome.

" 6th. On Captain Schenck's going out in the morning, we heard "the joyful sound of 'fair wind.' Set sail ; had a very light breeze ; "about noon wind sprang ahead ; beat down as far as New Baltimore ; "lowered sail, went on shore ; in the lime-kiln saw many curiosities. "Lay all night there.

" 7th. Set sail in the morning ; made one mile, and forced to lower "sail ; P. and I with great difficulty got on shore ; frightened on "board with the sight of a snake six feet long. About eleven o'clock "set sail ; after getting into the Highlands had a fair wind ; very "sick ; in Tappan Bay most delightful sailing ; went to bed about "dark ; could not sleep for thinking of getting to New York ; reached "there between ten and eleven o'clock. — Seven days from Albany."

"see their new minister at their respective houses, I was
"often tempted to spend days in visiting when I ought
"to be otherwise employed. After pursuing this course
"for four months, relying on my old stock, I found I
"had economized time to write only ten sermons.
"Under the deep conviction that this would not answer,
"I performed an act which, from the benefits resulting,
"I can recommend to every young minister upon chang-
"ing his field of labor. Taking out all my old sermons,
"to the number of three hundred and fifty, and having
"selected about a score, as specimens of my early essays
"at sermonizing, I made a bonfire of the residue. It
"was the noblest act, on my own behalf, I had ever per-
"formed, and I presume it was no less beneficial to the
"world. This act imposed on me the necessity of devot-
"ing three or four days in each week exclusively to
"study, as I had formed the determination not to be a
"sluggard in the Lord's Vineyard."

Mr. Prime devoted himself with assiduous care to
the education of his children, and in doing so acquired
wisdom from experience. His two earliest born were
started like hot-house plants, being taught to read before they were three years of age, and early advanced
in the study of the ancient languages and in science.
After these experiments he became convinced that he
had committed an error in forcing their tender minds
at too early an age, and his younger children were not
allowed to open a book or even to learn the alphabet
until they were five years old. He was inclined to
defer the commencement of their school education to a
still later period.

In the course of a few years, with an increasing

family to be reared and educated, and with a salary not at all commensurate with his enlarged expenses, he was induced in 1821 to accept the charge, as Principal, of the Washington Academy at Cambridge, — an institution which for many years had been sending out into the world a large number of influential men. This afforded him an opportunity immediately to superintend the education of his own children, to send his five sons to college, to sustain them through their entire course, and to give a liberal education to his two daughters. He tendered to his congregation his resignation of his pastorate; but it was declined, and for several years he continued to discharge the duties of both offices.

Throughout his life he preserved and cultivated the scholarly tastes of his youth. He was an accomplished Greek and Latin scholar, delighting to find rest and refreshment from arduous labor in reading the ancient classics in the original languages, or in hearing them read by his children.

He became an enthusiast in electrical science, constructing with his own hands for his laboratory, batteries and apparatus, with which he spent much time in experimenting. He was accustomed to prophesy in his public lectures and in his family, more than sixty years ago, that the time would come when electricity would do all the lighting, warming, and cooking work of civilization, and drive its engines also. At that time there was in the city of Albany a young watchmaker, named Henry, with whom Mr. Prime became acquainted in the ordinary way of his business. He was a friend of the Rev. Dr. Peter Bullions, the eminent Greek scholar who was Principal of the Albany Academy and an intimate friend of Mr. Prime. Finding that young Henry had devoted much attention to the subject of electricity and magnetism, and had made some remarkable experiments, Mr. Prime cultivated the acquaintance, which ripened into a life-long friendship. Impressed with his extraordinary capabilities and attainments, Mr. Prime joined with Dr. Bullions in urging him to bring out his discoveries in a public lecture, and promised, if he would do so, to drive from Cambridge to Albany, a distance of thirty-five miles, to hear him. The result was the first appearance before the public of the eminent Joseph Henry, who was successively professor in the Albany Academy and in Princeton College, and still later Secretary of the Smithsonian Institute. The present writer (though at that time a mere lad) remembers well the enthusiasm with which his father, on his return from Albany, detailed the lecture, described the experiments, and entered at once upon their repetition in his own small laboratory.

An incident that occurred soon after the commencement of Mr. Prime's ministry at Cambridge shows his early and efficient interest in the cause of foreign missions. The first missionaries to the Holy Land appointed by the American Board were Levi Parsons and Pliny Fisk. On completing his studies at Andover Theological Seminary in 1818, Mr. Parsons was appointed by the Board to spend a year visiting the churches, to awaken an interest in the cause, and to collect money for the Board, which was then in its infancy, and greatly in need of funds for sending out and supporting its missionaries. He spent several weeks among the churches of Vermont, but met with little success. One evening he came, a stranger, to the house of Mr. Prime, greatly discouraged with his failure, having collected in the State of Vermont only $155. By his gentle manners and Christian spirit he won the hearts of the pastor and his household, including his young children who have never ceased to cherish his memory with tender affection. The writer, who was then just four years old, has the most vivid recollection of this man of God and of many of the incidents of his visit.

On the following Sabbath, December 20, Mr. Parsons preached on the subject of his mission to the Holy Land, and made a deep impression upon the people. His appeal was warmly seconded by the pastor, and liberally responded to by the congregation. As he was about leaving the place, the pastor of a Scotch Presbyterian Church in the same town called upon the missionary and asked him to visit some of his people and present the cause to them personally. The result was that Mr. Parsons left Cambridge inspired with fresh hope and taking with him $505, contributed at this place to the funds of the Board. This was a remarkable offering to the cause for that day; nor was it an evanescent expression of interest on the part of Mr. Prime and his church. The work of missions continued to call forth their prayers and their liberal contributions, and the monthly concert of prayer for missions became one of the most interesting meetings of that church.

Mr. Prime was constitutionally a reformer, — not a mere ideal, but a practical reformer. He allowed his reason and good sense to regulate his action; but in considering questions of duty he never took counsel from his fears, and in carrying out his conscientious convictions he conferred not with flesh and blood. He was one of the earliest pioneers in the temperance reformation. On entering the sacred ministry, long before there was any popular movement in this direction, he became convinced that intoxicating drinks were not necessary to the enjoyment of health and vigor, and he resolved personally to abstain. But in obedience to the laws of hospitality of that day the decanters were allowed to remain on his sideboard, and were in requisition at all social gatherings, not excepting ministerial. In the year 1811 the celebrated essay by Dr. Benjamin Rush, of Philadelphia, entitled " An Inquiry into the " effects of Ardent Spirits on the Human Body and " Mind," was distributed in the Presbyterian General Assembly, and a copy of it was put into the hands of Mr. Prime. It produced upon him such an impression that as he rose from its perusal he went to his sideboard, locked up his decanters, and never again " put " the bottle to his neighbor's lips." Under the inspiration of Dr. Rush's treatise he wrote a sermon from the passage in Proverbs : " Who hath woe ? Who hath sor- " row ? Who hath contentions ? Who hath babbling ? " Who hath wounds without cause? Who hath redness " of eyes ? They that tarry long at the wine ; they that " go to seek mixed wine," etc. This sermon he preached at the opening of the Presbytery of Long Island, Nov. 5, 1811. It produced a great sensation. Some of his ministerial brethren thought he was beside himself. One of them said : " Brother Prime is the youngest " member of the Presbytery, and does he presume to

"teach us old men on this subject?" The Presbytery
on the following day took up the matter, and after a
full discussion unanimously adopted the following
resolution: —

"*Resolved*, That hereafter *ardent spirits* and *wine*
"shall constitute no part of our entertainment at any
"of our public meetings; and that it be recommended
"to their churches not to treat Christian brethren or
"others with ardent spirits as a part of hospitality in
"friendly visits."

The Presbytery sent to the churches under its care a
pastoral letter on the same subject, which, according to
the records of the time, had a very salutary effect in
promoting a wholesome public sentiment in regard to
the evils of intemperance.[1] By a unanimous vote of
the Presbytery, Mr. Prime's sermon was published and
circulated on Long Island, and in some communities
led to the adoption of strictly temperance principles
and action. After his removal to Cambridge he took a
leading part in promoting the cause by its public advocacy, by the organization of temperance societies, by
writing for the public Press, and by his own consistent
personal example.

On the 4th of July, 1825, which opened the fiftieth
or jubilee year of the independence of the United
States, Mr. Prime delivered in his own pulpit at Cambridge a discourse on the subject of slavery, taking for
his text a passage from the Declaration of Independence: "We hold these truths to be self-evident, that
"all men are created equal; that they are endowed by

---

[1] A copy of this letter and the action taken by the Presbytery
may be found in the appendix to Prime's "History of Long Island."

"their Creator with certain inalienable rights ; that "among these are Life, Liberty, and the Pursuit of "Happiness." It was a calm but thorough discussion of the subject of American slavery, with all its wrongs and sins and perils to the country. The discourse was preached on a week-day to a large congregation, which immediately took measures for its publication. It was printed with the title, "The Year of Jubilee, "but not to Africans."

During his residence of eighteen years at Cambridge, Mr. Prime took a leading part in the religious and benevolent movements of the day, and was specially active in promoting the cause of popular education and sound learning. Here he was associated with a number of professional gentlemen, some of them graduates of the Scotch universities, who formed a club for classical and scientific study, and were largely instrumental, by public lectures and other means, in promoting widely in the community a taste for learning. He was a trustee of Middlebury College from 1822 to 1826, and of Williams College from 1826 to 1831, when, having removed to a distance, he resigned.

In the spring of 1830 he accepted an invitation to become Principal of the Mount Pleasant Academy at Sing-Sing on the Hudson, and also took charge of the Presbyterian Church, again performing this double service for several years. In 1831 he established at the same place a female seminary, which, under the immediate superintendence and instruction of his eldest daughter, afterward Mrs. A. P. Cumings, soon acquired a high reputation. The building occupied by this seminary was destroyed by fire in October, 1835, when the institution was removed to Newburgh, where it continued to flourish under the same direction.

On the night of May 17, 1849, Dr. and Mrs. Prime had a narrow escape from being buried alive in a watery grave. Intending to visit some friends at Ballston Spa, they left New York at evening in the steamer "Empire," bound for Troy. They retired to their berths about ten o'clock, and not long after were aroused by a sudden shock. The engine having stopped, they hastened on deck in their night clothing, to find a crowd of passengers in a state of alarm and confusion, which was increased on learning that there were several feet of water already in the cabin, but no one seemed to know what had happened. As the steamer was sinking, they were assisted, in some way they knew not how, to climb to the upper deck, from which they got on board a schooner loaded with lumber, — the vessel that had caused the disaster by running into the " Empire " in the darkness. The steamer almost immediately went down in deep water, with a number of the passengers confined in the cabin, between twenty and thirty of whom perished. The schooner continued to float, and Dr. and Mrs. Prime were taken off and landed at Newburgh, where they were supplied by friends with clothing. Taking a steamer that was passing down the river, Mrs. Prime was in New York again before morning, bringing to the family the first news of their peril and of their remarkable escape.

On retiring from active responsibility as an educator, Dr. Prime declined to accept a pastoral charge. He continued, as had always been his wont, to be diligent in business, devoting his time and energies largely to

gratuitous public service. He wrote much for the Press,
he performed missionary labor in various localities, he
occupied different pulpits in New York city, Brooklyn,
Newark, and other places, — in some cases for a year or
more, — preaching with as much vigor and acceptance
as in former years. Nor in fulfilling these engagements
did he draw upon his old stock of sermons, but continued to prepare for the pulpit as studiously and with as
much interest as in the earliest days of his ministry.

On the 21st of October, 1855 (the day succeeding the
fiftieth anniversary of the one on which he preached his
first sermon at Huntington, Long Island, his native
town), he preached at the same place and in the same
church a discourse commemorative of his ministerial
life. This was subsequently amplified for the benefit
of his children. The private portion of these reminiscences concluded as follows : —

"In closing this review I ought to record the peculiar
"goodness of God to me through a life and ministry ex-
"tended so far beyond the average of human existence
"on earth, and under circumstances of peculiar comfort
"and enjoyment. Trials I have had—and who has not?
"— but they have always appeared to me, not only
"smaller than my deserts, but lighter than those of
"others. It has been the prevailing sentiment of my
"heart that few have passed through as long a life as I
"have lived, and enjoyed as large a share of happiness as
"has been assigned to me by a kind Providence. I have
"been blessed with a family of children who have never
"dishonored their parentage; and the most of them have
"passed the meridian of life with qualifications and with
"a disposition to labor in the service of God and for the

"benefit of the world. Only one of them has been cut
"down by the way; and in that case we had the un-
"speakable consolation to believe that he had the honor
"of being the first of the family to be bid welcome to
"*his* Father's and *our* Father's house above."

During several of his later years Dr. Prime resided
in the city of Brooklyn. The last year he spent at the
country home of his son-in-law, Mr. A. P. Cumings, at
Mamaroneck. Almost from the period of his reaching
manhood he had anticipated a sudden death, having
had early and frequent intimations of a tendency to
apoplexy. More than once on this account he had been
advised for a brief season to suspend public service, and
especially pulpit labor. But such attacks soon passed
away. The end came in a different form, though not
less suddenly. On the 27th of March, 1856, he spent
the day writing a sermon, which he had commenced in
the morning, on a subject that had recently impressed
itself upon his mind, — "Love is the fulfilling of the
"law." He had nearly completed the sermon as the
daylight was passing away. Laying down his pen, he
spent the evening in cheerful conversation with the
family, and retired at his usual hour, apparently in
perfect health. About midnight he awoke and com-
plained of pain in the region of the heart. While his
wife and daughter were ministering to his relief, without a thought that his end was near, his heart suddenly
stood still, and his active, useful life was ended.

Dr. Prime was a man of fine personal appearance and
commanding presence. He had a clear, strong voice,
which added much to his power in the pulpit and in
deliberative assemblies. He was an easy extempora-

neous speaker, a forcible debater, with a ready flow of language, strongly argumentative in the pulpit as well as in debate, seldom indulging in rhetoric, and never employing it as a substitute for thought or logic. His preaching was "in simplicity and godly sincerity, not "with enticing words of man's wisdom, but in demon-"stration of the Spirit and of power." When he spoke on any occasion, no one who heard him was in any doubt as to what he meant; if it was on any controverted point, no one doubted on which side he stood. As a theologian his views were clear, and clearly expressed. He was not only firmly, but intelligently attached to the Presbyterian Church, in which he had his birth, — to its system of doctrine and form of government. As an expounder of Presbyterian law and order, and as an advocate in the church courts, he had no superior. His counsel was often sought in cases of discipline, and he was frequently appointed on commissions to determine difficult cases of ecclesiastical procedure.

The degree of S. T. D. was conferred on him in 1848 by Princeton College, — an honor which he accepted with pleasure, chiefly because it was conferred by his own Alma Mater.

Of his general character and bearing, the Rev. Dr. Sprague wrote in his "Annals of the American "Pulpit: " —

"I knew the venerable Dr. Prime quite well during "the latter years of his life, and always regarded him "as a noble specimen of a man and a minister. He had "a mind of uncommon force and discrimination; a noble "and generous spirit; simple and engaging manners; an "invincible firmness in adhering to his own convictions;

"an earnest devotion to the best interests of his fellow-
"men; an excellent talent for the pulpit; great tact at
"public business; and a remarkably graceful facility at
"mingling in a deliberative body. He inherited from
"his father and grandfather a taste for letters, which
"he cultivated through life and transmitted to his
"posterity."

His widow, Mrs. Julia Ann Prime, survived him
nearly eighteen years. After enjoying a serene old age,
cherished in the affections and homes of her children,
retaining her mental faculties unimpaired, and enjoying
bodily vigor and health to the last, she passed away from
earth peacefully, at the home of her daughter, Mrs. Cumings, at White Plains, August 24th, 1874. As in the
case of her husband, neither she nor any of her family
were anticipating her departure. She had a slight illness, from which she was apparently recovering. On
the morning of her decease she awoke bright and cheerful; without rising, she sat up for a short time in her
bed, and as she laid her head again upon the pillow,
she closed her eyes and repeated aloud the first words
of the simple prayer of her childhood: —

> "Now I lay me down to sleep,
> I pray the Lord my soul to keep;
> If I should die before I wake,
> I pray the Lord my soul to take."

While the words were yet on her lips, and before she
had finished, the prayer was answered; she had gone
to be "forever with the Lord."

The following notice of the decease of Mrs. Prime is
taken from the "Washington County Post," published at

Cambridge, N. Y., where she had spent nearly twenty
years of her life as a pastor's wife : —

" No son or daughter of the ' Old White Church ' during
" the pastorate of the distinguished Dr. Prime over that
" church ever failed to love, esteem, and — we had al-
" most said — to worship the subject of this obituary.
" Nature had vouchsafed to her in a remarkable degree
" the rare qualities of grace and beauty.   These, together
" with richly endowed and highly cultivated powers, en-
" abled her to wield an influence that few of her sex can
" claim, and the impress of which is indelibly stamped
" upon the moral and religious character of not a few in
" our community unto the third and fourth generation.
" She was permitted to live and witness her family of
" sons and daughters grow up and take rank among
" the most distinguished scientific and literary men and
" women of the land, all of whom, we doubt not, will
" prove bright stars in her crown of rejoicing."

The children of NATHANIEL SCUDDER PRIME and
JULIA ANN JERMAIN, his wife, were, —

MARIA MARGARETTA, born at Sag Harbor, Long
Island, Aug. 14, 1809 ;

ALANSON JERMAIN, born at Smithtown, Long Island,
March 12, 1811 ; died at White Plains, N. Y., April 3,
1864.

SAMUEL IRENÆUS, born at Ballston, N. Y., Nov. 4,
1812 ; died at Manchester, Vt., July 18, 1885.

EDWARD DORR GRIFFIN, born at Cambridge, N. Y.,
Nov. 2, 1814.

CORNELIA, born at Cambridge, N. Y., Nov. 29, 1816.

GERRIT WENDELL, born at Cambridge, N. Y., July 13, 1819 ; died at Hudson, N. Y., April 12, 1837.

WILLIAM COWPER, born at Cambridge, N. Y., Oct. 31, 1825.

PUBLICATIONS OF REV. NATHANIEL S. PRIME, D.D.

A COLLECTION OF HYMNS, Original and Select, for the use of Small Assemblies and Private Christians. By Nathaniel S. Prime, Sag Harbor. Printed by Alden Spooner. 1809. pp. 139.

THE PERNICIOUS EFFECTS OF INTEMPERANCE in the use of Ardent Spirits, and the Remedy for that Evil. A SERMON delivered at the Opening of the Presbytery of Long Island at Aquebogue, Nov. 5, 1811. By Nathaniel S. Prime. (Published by Request.) Brooklyn : Printed by Alden Spooner. 1812. pp. 40.

AN ADDRESS to the Cambridge Branch of the Moral Society of the County of Washington. Delivered Sept. 11, 1815. By Nathaniel S. Prime, Pastor of the Presbyterian Church in Cambridge (N. Y.). Albany : Printed by Churchill Abbey, No. 95 State Street, Five Doors east of the Episcopal Church. 1815. pp. 24.

A PLAN for the more Successful Management of Domestic Missions, in a Letter to a Friend. By an Evangelist. Albany : Printed by Henry C. Southwick, No. 94 State Street. 1816. pp. 23.

DIVINE TRUTH the Established Means of Sanctification : A SERMON, Delivered at the Annual Meeting of the Washington County Bible Society, N. Y., in South Granville, Jan. 29, 1817. By Nathaniel S. Prime, Pastor of the Presbyterian Church in Cambridge, N. Y. Salem : Printed by Dodd & Stevenson, at the Salem Bookstore. 1817. pp. 32.

A FAMILIAR ILLUSTRATION OF CHRISTIAN BAPTISM, in which the Subjects of that Ordinance and the Mode of Administration are ascertained from the Word of God and the History of the Church; and defended from the Objections usually urged by the Opposers of Infant Baptism and the Advocates of Immersion. In the Form of a Dialogue. By Nathaniel S. Prime, Pastor of the Presbyterian Church in Cambridge, N. Y. Salem, N. Y.; Printed by Dodd & Stevenson. 1818. pp. 312.

ADDRESS to the Congregation at the Ordination of Absalom Peters as Pastor of the Congregation Church at Bennington, Vt., July 5th, 1820.

THE YEAR OF JUBILEE, BUT NOT TO AFRICANS: A Discourse delivered July 4th, 1825, Being the Forty-ninth Anniversary of American Independence. By Nathaniel S. Prime, Pastor of the First Presbyterian Church in Cambridge, N. Y. Salem: Printed by Dodd & Stevenson. 1825. pp. 24.

CHARGE to Rev. Samuel Irenæus Prime. Delivered at his Installation as Pastor of the First Presbyterian Church of Matteawan, in the Town of Fishkill, Dutchess County, N. Y., May 23, 1837. By Nathaniel S. Prime, Principal of the Newburgh Female Seminary. Newburgh: Printed by J. D. Spalding. 1837. pp. 22.

A HISTORY OF LONG ISLAND, from its First Settlement by Europeans, to the Year 1845, with Special Reference to its Ecclesiastical Concerns. In Two Parts. I. Its Physical Features and Civil Affairs. II. Annals of the Several Towns, relating chiefly to Ecclesiastical Matters. By Nathaniel S. Prime. New York: Robert Carter, 58 Canal Street; and Pittsburg, 56 Market Street. 1845. pp. 420.

MRS. MARIA M. CUMINGS.

MARIA MARGARETTA, eldest child of the Rev. Nathaniel S. Prime, D.D., and Julia Ann Jermain, his wife, was born at Sag Harbor, Long Island, Aug. 14, 1809. She early exhibited a decided taste for the study of languages, especially for the Latin and Greek; and before she was fifteen had made written translations of several of the ancient classic authors. After enjoying the advantages of the female department of the Washington Academy at Cambridge, she attended the school of Miss Gilbert at Albany, and completed her school education at the Troy Female Seminary under Mrs. Emma Willard, the distinguished pioneer in the higher education of women. This distinction has been claimed for other American teachers; but the institution which Mrs. Willard founded was by several years the first to offer to young women a complete education, and to fit them to become educators of their own sex in all the departments of useful learning. As the pioneer, and as an institution of a high order, it merits this recognition.

Inspired by the enthusiasm of her eminent instructress, and by her own desire for usefulness, Miss Prime devoted several years to the practical work of teaching others. At the age of fifteen she became an assistant to her father in the Cambridge Academy, and had under her immediate instruction advanced pupils, including a number of young men who were largely indebted to her for their preparation to enter college, and who in subsequent professional life made special acknowledgment of their obligations to her for laying the foundations of their classical education. Mention has been made in the preceding sketch of a club of literary and professional gentlemen who met regularly to revive their college and university studies, and especially to read familiarly their favorite Latin and Greek authors. Miss Prime's rare attainments in the languages secured for her a unanimous election as a member of this club, — a tribute which in no other case was accorded to one of her sex.

In 1831, in connection with her father, she established the Mount Pleasant Female Seminary at Sing Sing, in which, and after its removal to Newburgh, several hundred young ladies, from all parts of the country, were under her immediate instruction and training.

She was married, March 31, 1836, to Mr. A. P. Cumings, one of the editors and proprietors of the "New York Observer," who, after a life of great activity in this and other fields of usefulness, especially in the general work of Christian benevolence, died at Nice, France, May 13, 1871.

Mrs. Cumings contributed occasionally to the columns of the "New York Observer" and to other periodicals, and by urgent request she prepared two volumes for the press, — one the Memoirs of a missionary's daughter who had been providentially sent to her house to die; the other, a Memorial of a very dear friend. They were published anonymously.

The adopted child of A. P. Cumings and Maria M., his wife, was Cornelia Josephine, who was married to Mr. James L. Truslow.

PUBLICATIONS OF MRS. MARIA M. CUMINGS.

THE MISSIONARY'S DAUGHTER; or, Memoir of Lucy Goodale Thurston, of the Sandwich Islands. "Why "brought here to wither, but to fulfil some high behest "of Heaven?" New York: Dayton & Newman. 1842. pp. 223.

MEMORIAL OF MRS. CATHARINE ANN JERMAIN, who died April 21, 1873, wife of James B. Jermain, of Albany. Inscribed to her children and children's children and family friends, at the request of her husband. Munsell, Printer, Albany.

ALANSON JERMAIN PRIME, M.D.

ALANSON JERMAIN, eldest son of the Rev. Nathaniel S. Prime, D.D., and Julia Ann Jermain, his wife, was born at Smithtown, Long Island, March 12, 1811. He pursued his preparatory studies, under the immediate instruction of his father, at Cambridge, N. Y. In 1826 he entered the Sophomore class at Williams College, under the presidency of the Rev. Edward Dorr Griffin, D.D., and was graduated with honor in the class of 1829. Having the medical profession in view, he devoted special attention while in college to chemistry and natural science generally. After his graduation he continued his scientific studies at the Troy Rensselaer Institute (now the Polytechnic), under the instruction of Professor Eaton, then eminent as a naturalist. He subsequently delivered courses of public lectures, at Cambridge and other places, on his favorite subjects of study. He studied medicine with Dr. Matthew Stevenson, of Cambridge, and at Sing Sing with Dr. Adrian K. Hoffman, father of ex-Governor John K. Hoffman. He attended the courses of medical lectures at the College of Physicians and Surgeons in the city of New York. Soon after he received his medical license, in 1832, the Asiatic cholera made its appearance in this country. The first death at Quebec occurred on the 8th of June, 1832, and the first in the city of New York on the 22d of the same month. Spreading rapidly in all directions, but confined chiefly to cities and places where large masses of people were congregated, it broke out with great violence in the State Prison at Sing Sing. Dr. Prime was immediately appointed a special physician for the prison; and although the disease was regarded, even by many of the faculty, as highly contagious, he took up his residence at once within the walls of the prison, where he remained for several weeks, day and night, ready to attend upon any one who might be attacked, and to minister to those who were already suffering. Several hundred cases occurred, many prisoners being seized in their cells suddenly in the night. About one hundred of the cases proved fatal, but no one suffered for want of timely medical attendance.

A singular incident, worthy of special note, marked the sudden disappearance of the disease from that locality. While it was still prevailing in the prison, a violent thunderstorm broke over the place early one evening, and continued during a great part of the night. From that time not another new case of cholera occurred within the prison walls, and it soon disappeared. In other cases a similar result did not attend the same electrical phenomena.

Another incident, of a personal nature, connected with Dr. Prime's special service in this cholera hospital may here be mentioned. He was summoned one day to attend a prisoner, a young man, who had been violently attacked with the disease. After he had examined the case and had made prescription, the young man called him by name, and added, "Doctor, you do "not know me." Dr. Prime replied that he did not recognize him; on which the young man said, "We "were boys together at the Old White Meeting House "where your father preached." He was proceeding to relate the history of his life and of the way in which he had been brought to the prison, and, as he now feared, to the gate of death, when the Doctor stopped him in his narrative, directing him to remain perfectly quiet, as one of the necessary conditions of his recovery, and to tell him the story when he had more strength. He recovered, and subsequently gave the Doctor a history of his crime. He did not serve out the full term of his sentence, but was pardoned on the ground of his good conduct while in prison, and on the application of his former employers, who took him back into their service.

After practising medicine a short time at Schenectady, N. Y., Dr. Prime removed to Grand Haven, Mich., to pursue his profession; but he was soon broken down by continuous attacks of the fever of the new country, and returned to the East. On recovering his health he took charge, as Principal, of the Academy at Newburgh, and subsequently resumed practice for a year at Plattekill, Ulster County, N. Y. In 1848 he removed to White Plains, N. Y., where he continued in the successful practice of his profession until his death, which occurred April 3, 1864.

He married, Sept. 1, 1836, Ruth, youngest daughter of Benjamin Higbie, of Troy, N. Y. Their children were Ralph Earl, Mary, Katharine, Margaretta, married to Henry C. Bissell, and Alanson Jermain,—all now living.

PUBLICATIONS OF ALANSON J. PRIME, M.D.

Dr. A. J, Prime commenced while very young, and continued to the close, to use his pen both as a prose writer and as a poet, contributing largely to the periodical Press. Among the papers which he furnished for "Harper's Magazine" were, "Insects and Insect Life;" "Coincidences;" "Mary Rankin: A Physician's Story;" "Why our Minister didn't Marry;" "Paul Allen's Wife, and how He found Her;" "Fortune-Telling;" "The Sheriff's Wife." For the "Christian Parlor Magazine" he furnished "Passages in the Life of a Physician;" "Our First-born;" and for the "Columbian Magazine," "Eunice Marston."

In 1845, in connection with Professor Emmons, his former instructor at Williams College, and State Geologist of New York, he established a Scientific Magazine of Agriculture, which was continued through two volumes under the following title:—

AMERICAN QUARTERLY JOURNAL OF AGRICULTURE AND SCIENCE. Edited by Dr. E. Emmons and Dr. A. J. Prime. Albany: Van Benthuysen & Co. 1845.

SAMUEL IRENÆUS PRIME, D.D.

SAMUEL IRENÆUS, second son of Rev. Nathaniel S. Prime, D.D., and Julia Ann Jermain, his wife, was born at Ballston, N. Y., Nov. 4, 1812. His early education was conducted by his father at the Cambridge Washington Academy. In October, 1826, with his older brother, he entered the Sophomore class in Williams College, and was graduated in 1829, before he had completed his seventeenth year, taking one of the four honors of the class, — the Greek Oration. He spent three years after his graduation in teaching at Cambridge and Sing Sing, when he entered Princeton Theological Seminary. Before completing his first year he had a severe illness, by which he was brought to the borders of the grave. His parents and other members of his family were summoned to his bedside, not expecting his recovery, nor was he able afterward to resume his studies at Princeton. He was licensed to preach by the Presbytery of Bedford in 1833, and the same year took charge of the Academy at Weston, Conn.

On the 15th of October, 1833, he married Elizabeth Thornton, daughter of the Hon. Edward Kemeys, of Sing Sing. She died Aug. 9, 1834, a few days after giving birth to a son, who was named Samuel Thornton Kemeys.

In 1835 Mr. Prime accepted a call to the Presbyterian Church of Ballston Spa, and in June of that year was ordained and installed its first pastor. On the 17th of August, 1835, he married Eloisa Lemet, daughter of Mr. Moses Williams, of Ballston Spa. His pastorate at this place gave great promise of usefulness; but before the completion of a year a serious bronchial ailment, from which he never fully recovered, developed itself, and he was compelled to resign his charge and resort again to teaching. He became Principal of the Academy at Newburgh, N. Y., and after two years, being in a measure relieved, he returned to the work of the ministry. Accepting a call to the Presbyterian Church at Matteawan, N. Y., he was installed May 23, 1837. He often referred to his pastorate of three years at this place as one of the happiest periods of his life. It was marked by hard labor, but was attended with rich fruits. In the spring of 1840 he was compelled by the state of his health again to give up preaching, when he entered upon the chief work of his life, accepting the editorship of the "New York Observer." This he never laid aside excepting during an interval of a year in which he was one of the Secretaries of the American Bible Society, and a few months in which he was connected with the "Presbyterian." Never did any one find employment for which he was more admirably fitted, or in which he achieved greater success. He wrote with as much ease as he talked, and with such accuracy that his articles were sent to the printer with little, often with no revision. The writer of these notes, after intimate association with his brother in editorial work between thirty and forty years, can truly say that he never knew another who wrote with equal celerity, precision, and force, and whom it apparently cost so little effort. When he had performed a day's work in the office or in his study, he was ready to take up some service in behalf of one of the numerous benevolent enterprises of the day with which he was identified, or to sit down again and write an article for some periodical, or prepare a portion of a volume or a public address. It was in this way, not as a task, but as the overflow of an ever active and never weary mind that he was enabled, while discharging his regular editorial duties, to prepare for the press more than forty volumes, besides pamphlets, addresses, tracts, and scores of articles for reviews and magazines.

In April, 1853, being broken down in health, he sailed for Europe to spend a year in travel, should his life and strength be spared so long. He was so feeble when carried to the ship that he was laid almost helpless upon the deck. He was revived by the air of the sea, and on reaching the other shore was so much invigorated that he entered at once upon an extensive tour on the continent of Europe and in Palestine and Egypt. He returned home at the end of a year with restored health, having lost scarcely a day by illness. He made a second visit to Europe in 1866-7, and a third in 1876-7. In all his travels he contributed weekly to the "Observer," under his familiar signature of "IRENÆUS," a series of letters which was never intermitted until it was broken off by his death.

The degree of D.D. was conferred on him by Hampden Sidney College.

Soon after entering upon his editorial work, Dr.

Prime took up his residence for a few years in the city of Newark, N. J., where he attended the Third Presbyterian Church, then under the pastoral care of the Rev. Dr. H. N. Brinsmade. He took the superintendence of the Sunday-school, in which he did the work of a pastor, and was also active in promoting the general work of the church. He bore a prominent part in establishing the Public Library of Newark, and was engaged in other local and public enterprises. He was a living as well as life-member and director of numerous national, Christian, and philanthropic societies, and found leisure to devote to them all. His time and energies were long and heartily given to the Evangelical Alliance, on which for many years he expended without compensation a vast amount of labor as one of its corresponding-secretaries. He was the founder and president of the New York Association for the Advancement of Science and Art, of which (it is not too much to say) he was the life and soul; president and trustee of Wells College; a trustee of Williams College, etc.

During all the later years of his life Dr. Prime had his residence in the city of New York. In the summer of 1885 he left the city to fulfil an engagement to preach in the Presbyterian Church at Ballston Spa on the 7th of June, the fiftieth anniversary of his ordination in that church.[1] On the 1st of July he attended the Commencement of Williams College, and went

---

[1] A memorial-window representing the Resurrection of our Lord, a copy of the design by Albert Dürer in his series known as "The "Great Passion," has been placed by his widow in this church over the pulpit. The text of the sermon preached on the occasion referred to is added as a legend: "Blessed are the pure in heart, for they shall "see God."

thence to Manchester, Vt., to make arrangements to
spend the month of August at that place with his
family, and to celebrate with them the fiftieth anniversary of his marriage. He was taken ill on the way,
and immediately on reaching Manchester summoned
a physician. He was soon after joined by his wife
and other members of the family. There was nothing
alarming in the attack, and for several days he continued to improve.

On Sunday morning, July 12, as his physician, Dr.
Hemenway, was leaving the room to attend public
worship, Dr. Prime asked him to wait a moment, and
attempted to utter a request; but his voice faltered,
and he said to his brother, William C. Prime, "Give
"me the pencil and paper." He then wrote the following, which he desired the doctor to hand to the pastor
at the church: —

"To THE PASTOR: A stranger in town, being ill,
"desires the congregation to unite with him in thanks
"to God for his goodness in partially restoring him,
"and in praying for complete recovery."

And he added (for the pastor alone), "No name to
"be mentioned."

In the course of the day, at intervals, he engaged in
conversation with his wife and brother on various
topics of religious interest. In the afternoon he sat
up for some time, and at length, with a firm step,
walked to the bed, and lying down, closed his eyes and
apparently fell asleep. The doctor entered soon after,
and approaching the bedside, spoke to him, but received
no answer. He had been stricken with paralysis, and
never spoke again.

He lingered in this condition, suffering no pain and giving no signs of consciousness, until Saturday, the 18th, when he passed away so quietly that it was impossible to tell at what moment his spirit took its flight to join the company of the redeemed.

His funeral was attended, on the 22d, at the West Presbyterian Church, New York city. Addresses were made by his pastor, the Rev. Dr. John R. Paxton, and the Rev. Dr. Thomas S. Hastings, and prayer was offered by the Rev. Dr. William Ormiston. The burial was at Woodlawn Cemetery.

So many of the friends and associates of Dr. Prime were absent from the city and from the country at the time of his death that the Evangelical Alliance, of which he was a conspicuous member, resolved to hold at a later day a public commemorative meeting. Accordingly, on the 5th of January following, by invitation of the Alliance, a large assembly was gathered at Association Hall. William E. Dodge, Esq., president of the United States Alliance, presided, and opened the exercises with an appropriate address. Prayer was offered by the Rev. A. C. Wedekind, D.D., of the Lutheran Church, and a paper which had been adopted by the Council of the British Evangelical Alliance, expressive of their sorrow on hearing of the decease of Dr. Prime, was read by the Rev. Philip Schaff, D.D. Eloquent and impressive addresses were then made by the Rev. Drs. Richard S. Storrs of the Congregational Church, Edward Bright of the Baptist Church, and James M. Buckley of the Methodist Episcopal Church.

His general character and manner of life are portrayed in a tribute to his memory by the Rev. Dr.

T. W. Chambers, of the Collegiate Reformed Dutch
Church, published at the time of his death, from which
we make an extract: —

"He was a man of public spirit and a constant friend
"of the great religious and benevolent and educational
"institutions of the age. His zeal was bounded by no
"narrow or sectarian lines. Whether it were a Bible
"or a Tract Society, in the interest of Home Missions
"or of Foreign, for a college or a seminary, for the
"Evangelical Alliance or that of the Reformed Churches,
"for the advancement of literature or of science or
"of art, he was ready to render such service as lay
"in his power. And his position often enabled him
"to give very efficient aid both by his voice and his
"pen. His spirit was truly catholic. Although warmly
"attached to the Evangelical system as held by the
"church in which he was reared and in whose com-
"munion his whole life was spent, he habitually cher-
"ished a hearty sympathy with all sister churches.
"And this feeling grew with his advancing years. He
"preferred to see points of agreement rather than those
"of difference, and longed for the closer fellowship of
"all who 'hold the Head.' Hence when the proposal
"was made to reunite the dissevered parts of the Pres-
"byterian Church North, he became at once a zealous
"and a judicious advocate of the reunion; and when
"the project was consummated, no man rejoiced more
"heartily than he. So when fraternal relations with
"the Southern Church were restored, he was a member
"of the commission which met the Southern Assembly
"at Lexington, Ky. His address on that occasion is
"said by one who was present to have been of great

" power through its tenderness. 'He spoke of the past,
"' and conjured up its sacred memories so that old men
"' wept.' "

Of his social characteristics Dr. Chambers writes :

" Dr. Prime's intercourse with his ministerial brethren
" was always pleasant and helpful. It was a great grat-
" ification to him when, cut off from the possibility of
" having a pulpit of his own, he was able to render
" service on occasion to those who required aid in ful-
" filling their office. In advanced years the state of
" his health prevented this from being often done ; but
" it rarely hindered him from attending the weekly
" gatherings of a clerical association in this city, now
" more than half a century old. Here his presence was
" a conspicuous and most agreeable feature. He never
" seemed out of spirits. His good-humor was pervading
" and infectious. His recollections of men and things
" were so vivid and so ready, and his knowledge of
" affairs so complete and accurate, that no subject was
" ever started on which he could not throw some needed
" light. His wit coruscated, his playfulness was ex-
" uberant, yet never excessive. In the greatest mirth,
" or in reciting the most amusing incident, he never
" forgot the dignity of a Christian minister."

The children of the Rev. S. Irenæus Prime, D.D.,
and Eloisa Lemet Williams, his wife, were Wendell,
Mary Elizabeth, married to the Rev. Charles A. Stod-
dard, D.D., Edward Irenæus, who died Oct. 29, 1849,
and Lily.

PUBLICATIONS OF REV. S. IRENÆUS PRIME, D.D.

To say that Dr. Prime was a voluminous writer, is to give little idea of the number and variety of the productions of his pen, or of their wide circulation. In addition to his weekly writings in the "New York Observer," continued for nearly half a century, and his contributions to numerous other periodicals, he was constantly called upon to prepare papers for religious, benevolent, and literary societies and objects. Besides volumes of sermons and other selections which he edited, the following list is made up from original volumes which were written chiefly in the midst of other arduous labors. No attempt has been made to catalogue the numerous articles which he prepared for magazines and reviews. Several of his volumes were reprinted and extensively circulated in foreign countries. After nearly twenty thousand copies of one of his books on Prayer had been published in this country, it was reprinted in England, where one hundred thousand copies were sold by a single publishing house. Two distinct translations of the same book were published in France ; it was issued from the press in India in the Tamil language, and in Dutch at the Cape of Good Hope.

ELIZABETH THORNTON : The Flower and Fruit of Early Piety. New York: M. W. Dodd. 1840. pp. 208.

RECORDS OF A VILLAGE PASTOR. Massachusetts Sabbath-School Society. 1843. pp. 228.

THE PRODIGAL RECLAIMED ; or, The Sinner's Ruin and Recovery. Mass. S. S. Society. 1843. pp. 220.

THE MARTYR MISSIONARY OF ERROMANGA; or, The Life
of John Williams. Abridged. American Sunday-School
Union. 1844. pp. 270.

THE LITTLE BURNT GIRL: A Memoir of Catharine Howell.
Am. S. S. Union. 1845. pp. 69.

GEORGE SOMERVILLE; or, The Boy who would be a
Minister. Am. S. S. Union. 1846. pp. 88.

GUIDE TO THE SAVIOUR. Am. S. S. Union. 1846.
pp. 96. (Republished by the London Religious Tract
Society.)

THE OLD WHITE MEETING-HOUSE; or, Reminiscences
of a Country Congregation. Robert Carter. 1846. pp.
240.

LIFE IN NEW YORK. Robert Carter & Brothers. 1846.
pp. 240.

THE GOSPEL AMONG THE BECHUANAS and other Tribes
of Southern Africa. Am. S. S. Union. 1846. pp. 296.

THE NESTORIANS OF PERSIA; with an Account of the
Massacres by the Koords. Am. S. S. Union. 1846. pp.
173.

THE HIGHLAND PASTOR: a Sequel to George Somerville.
pp. 197. Am. S. S. Union. 1847. pp. 197.

HENRY WOOD; or, The First Step in the Downward
Road. Am. S. S. Union. 1848. pp. 144.

BOSSES AND THEIR BOYS; or, The Duties of Masters
and Apprentices. Am. S. S. Union. 1853. pp. 144.

SABBATH SONGS: for the Use of Families and Sunday-
Schools. Leavitt & Allen. 1853.

THOUGHTS ON THE DEATH OF LITTLE CHILDREN; with
an Appendix selected from Various Authors. Anson D.
F. Randolph. 1865. pp. 180.

TRAVELS IN EUROPE AND THE EAST. With engravings.
Two vols. 12mo, pp. 405, 444. Harper & Brothers. 1855.
LETTERS FROM SWITZERLAND. Sheldon & Co. 1860.
pp. 264.

THE POWER OF PRAYER Illustrated in the Fulton-Street
Prayer Meetings and Elsewhere. Charles Scribner: New
York. 1858. The same, enlarged edition, Scribner, Arm-
strong & Co. 1873. pp. 418. The same, republished
in London; in Paris, in French, 1859; in Cape of Good
Hope, in Dutch; in East Indies, in Tamil.

THE BIBLE IN THE LEVANT; or, The Life and Letters
of the Rev. C. N. Righter, agent of the American Bible
Society in the Levant. New York: Sheldon & Co. 1859.
pp. 336.

FIVE YEARS OF PRAYER, with the Answers. Harper
& Brothers. 1864. pp. 395.

FIFTEEN YEARS OF PRAYER in the Fulton-Street Meeting. Scribner, Armstrong & Co. 1872. pp. 345.

AMERICAN WIT AND HUMOR. Harper & Brothers. 1859.
pp. 206.

ANDERSON'S ANNALS OF THE ENGLISH BIBLE. Abridged
and continued. Robert Carter & Brothers. 1849. pp.
545.

MEMOIRS OF REV. NICHOLAS MURRAY, D.D. (Kirwan).
Harper & Brothers. 1862. pp. 438.

MEMOIRS OF MRS. JOANNA BETHUNE. By her Son, Rev.
George W. Bethune, D.D. With an Appendix containing
Extracts from her Writings. Selected and edited by S. I. P.
Harper & Brothers. 1863. pp. 250.

WALKING WITH GOD: The Life Hid with Christ. A.
D. F. Randolph & Co. 1872. Republished in London,
1872.

THE ALHAMBRA AND THE KREMLIN: The South and
the North of Europe contrasted. A. D. F. Randolph &
Co. 1873. pp. 482.

UNDER THE TREES. Harper & Brothers. 1874. pp.
313.

SONGS OF THE SOUL Gathered out of Many Lands and
Ages. Robert Carter & Brothers. 1874. 4to. pp. 661.

HISTORY OF THE SIXTH GENERAL CONFERENCE OF THE
EVANGELICAL ALLIANCE. Harper & Brothers. 1874. pp.
773.

LIFE OF S. F. B. MORSE, LL.D., Inventor of the Electric
Magnetic Recording Telegraph. D. Appleton & Co. 8vo.
pp. 776.

IRENÆUS LETTERS: Originally published in the "New
York Observer." Published by the "New York Observer."
Series I., 1880; pp. 400. Series II., 1885, with a sketch
of the life of Rev. S. Irenæus Prime, D.D., pp. 388.

PRAYER AND ITS ANSWER, Illustrated in the Twenty-five
Years of the Fulton-Street Prayer-Meeting. Charles Scribner's Sons. 1882. pp. 171.

Among his public addresses, which were separately
published, are, "Address at the Opening of the Newark
Library Building, Feb. 21, 1848;" "Presbyterianism in
the United States of America," read at the Presbyterian
General Council, Edinburgh, July, 1877; "The Church
of Rome," a speech in the Presbyterian General Assembly,
Saratoga, May 26, 1879; "Address on the Erection of
the Franklin Statue, Printing-House Square, New York,
Jan. 17, 1872;" "Address before the British Organization
of the Evangelical Alliance, Bath, England, October,
1866;" etc., etc.

REV. EDWARD D. G. PRIME, D.D.

[This Sketch was prepared by William C. Prime, LL.D.]

EDWARD DORR GRIFFIN, third son of the Rev. Nathaniel S. Prime, D.D., and Julia Ann Jermain, his wife, was born at Cambridge, N. Y., Nov. 2, 1814. In common with his older brothers, he received his preparatory education at the Washington Academy in his native town, under the immediate instruction of his father. He entered Union College during the presidency of the Rev. Eliphalet Nott, D.D., who was then in his full vigor and celebrity as an educator. He was graduated in 1832, in his eighteenth year, taking one of the honors of his class, — the Latin oration. The Asiatic cholera making its appearance in this country in June of that year, the College was almost entirely disbanded, but the Commencement exercises were held in the midst of the pestilence.

After his graduation he spent three years in teaching, as an assistant to his father, in the Mount Pleasant Academy. He commenced the study of medicine under Dr. Adrian K. Hoffman, then surgeon of the State Prison at Sing Sing; but in the autumn of 1835 he decided to devote his life to the Christian ministry, and entered the Theological Seminary at Princeton. After

a three years' course at this institution he was graduated in the class of 1838, and was licensed to preach,
May 16th of that year, by the Presbytery of North
River. In December he was called to become an
assistant to the Rev. Methuselah Baldwin, pastor of
the Presbyterian Church of Scotchtown, Orange County,
N. Y., and was ordained collegiate pastor June 12, 1839.
On the death of Mr. Baldwin, Feb. 27, 1847, he became
sole pastor. On the 26th of September, 1839, he married Maria Darlington, daughter of John S. Wilson, of
Princeton, N. J. In the autumn of 1849, while he was
on his way to fulfil an appointment of Presbytery in
a distant church, he was attacked a second time with
hemorrhage of the lungs, but after a brief period of rest
he continued to discharge the duties of his pastorate.
In November, 1850, accompanied by his wife, he went
to New Orleans to spend the winter, for the benefit of
his health. On arriving there he accepted an invitation to supply the pulpit of the Lafayette Square
Presbyterian Church for six months, during the absence of the pastor, the Rev. William A. Scott, D.D.,
who was then travelling in Palestine and Egypt. The
following May he left New Orleans to attend the meeting of the Presbyterian General Assembly at St. Louis
as a commissioner from the Presbytery of Hudson.
While he was on the Mississippi the cholera made its
appearance on the steamer, and several deaths occurred.
Mrs. Prime was suddenly attacked, and within twenty-
four hours from the appearance of the first symptoms
the disease had passed through all its stages. She died
on the steamer " Iowa," May 13, 1851.

The following winter Mr. Prime, still suffering from

the effects of hemorrhage of the lungs, resigned his pastoral charge and went to Augusta, Ga. On returning to the North in May, he took charge of the Presbyterian Church in Eighty-sixth Street, New York, for a year. In April, 1853, to enable his brother Irenæus to recruit his health by foreign travel, he took his place as editor of the " New York Observer," with which paper he had corresponded for many years under the signature of " EUSEBIUS." After the return of his brother they were associated in editorial labor until the death of Irenæus, in 1885. He spent the winter of 1854–55, in Rome, officiating as chaplain of the American Embassy, under the appointment of the American and Foreign Christian Union. The following summer he travelled extensively in Europe, returning to New York in October, and resuming his duties on the " Observer."

In 1857 he received the degree of D.D. from Jefferson College, Pennsylvania. On the 14th of June, 1860, he married Abbie Davis, daughter of the Rev. William Goodell, D.D., of Constantinople. In 1869, being again broken down in health, and under the necessity of seeking complete relaxation from care and labor, he left home with Mrs. Prime on a journey around the world. Crossing the American continent by the Pacific Railroad, then just opened, he visited California, and on the 7th of September sailed from San Francisco for Japan and China. He spent the following winter in India, and in 1870 returned to New York by way of Egypt, Palestine, and Europe, having made the circuit of the globe. One special object that he had in view in selecting this extended route of travel, was to study in person the religious condition of those remote countries, and especially to note the progress of the work of Christian missions in the East. While absent, he corresponded regularly with the " New York Observer." On his return he published a volume containing an account of his travels and observations, which passed through several editions. He also preached and lectured on the missionary aspects of his journey in many of the churches of New York, Philadelphia, and other cities, presenting a hopeful view of the great work of Christianizing the nations.

In common with his editorial associates and others connected with the " New York Observer," he narrowly escaped death in the disastrous fire by which the " Observer " building, with its contents, was destroyed, and in which three of the compositors perished. Hearing the alarm of fire, he sprang to the door of his room, on the third story of the building, but turned back for an instant to secure some valuable papers. The whole interior was at once in flames ; and no other way being open, he stepped out of the window, and walking along the edges of the signs, reached a window in the adjoining building, and in this way made his escape.

On the death of his brother Irenæus, in 1885, he became editor-in-chief of the " Observer," the duties of which position he continued to perform until the following year, when, owing to repeated attacks of illness, he was compelled to resign the responsibilities and labors of the office.

PUBLICATIONS OF REV. E. D. G. PRIME, D.D.

Besides contributing largely to several volumes which were issued without his name, Dr. Prime published the following: —

AROUND THE WORLD: Sketches of Travel Through Many Lands and Over Many Seas. With numerous Illustrations. Harper & Brothers. 1872. Crown 8vo. pp. 455.

FORTY YEARS IN THE TURKISH EMPIRE; OR, MEMOIRS OF REV. WILLIAM GOODELL, D.D., Late Missionary of the A. B. C. F. M. at Constantinople. Robert Carter & Brothers. 1876. Crown 8vo. pp. 489.

(Calvinism and Missions) AN ADDRESS before the Synod of New York, Oct. 19, 1852. Foreign Missionary, January, 1853.

Civil and Religious Liberty in Turkey. Presbyterian Quarterly and Princeton Review, October, 1875.

NOTES, GENEALOGICAL, BIOGRAPHICAL, AND BIBLIO-GRAPHICAL, OF THE PRIME FAMILY. 8vo. 1888. Printed for Private Use. pp. 118.

MRS. CORNELIA P. STEVENSON.

CORNELIA, second daughter of the Rev. Nathaniel S. Prime, D.D., and Julia Ann Jermain, his wife, was born at Cambridge, N. Y., Nov. 29, 1816. Educated under her father and her elder sister, she spent several years in teaching, as an assistant in the institution of which they had charge, the Mount Pleasant Female Seminary. On the 18th of May, 1841, she was married to the Rev. Paul Eugene Stevenson, pastor of the Presbyterian Church at Staunton, Va., and removed immediately to that place. In 1844 her husband was called to the pastorate of the Presbyterian Church at Williamsburg, N. Y. (now the eastern division of Brooklyn), where they remained until 1849. In that year he accepted a call to the Presbyterian Church at Wyoming, Pa., and at the same time took charge of the Luzerne Presbyterian Institute. He was Principal successively of classical schools in Bridgeton and Madison, N. J. In 1866 Mr. and Mrs. Stevenson founded, in the city of Paterson, N. J., the Passaic Falls Institute for Young Ladies, in which he remained until his death, which occurred March 17, 1870, after which Mrs. Stevenson presided over the institution for several years.

Their children were Julia Johnson (died March 5, 1854), James Prime (died Nov. 21, 1860), Archibald Alexander (died Feb. 10, 1870), Preston, Eugene, Mary Margaretta, and Edward Irenæus.

Mrs. Stevenson has sustained the literary reputation of the family by her contributions to the periodical Press, among which was a series of articles published in the "New York Observer," under the title of "THE ALMOND TREE ; or, Conversations on the Twelfth Chapter of Ecclesiastes : 1874."

GERRIT WENDELL PRIME.

GERRIT WENDELL, fourth son of the Rev. Nathaniel S. Prime, D.D., and Julia Ann Jermain his wife, was born at Cambridge, N. Y., July 13, 1819. He received his early education at the same institutions with his brothers, and entered the Sophomore class in Union College in 1835. During his college course he suffered much from ill health, but maintained a high stand in his class. At the close of the winter session in his Junior year he left college to spend the vacation at home, taking the steamer at Albany for New York. The river was just breaking up, and the boat becoming imbedded in the ice, young Prime, together with several of his college mates who were on board, with great effort and difficulty made his way to the shore on the loose cakes of ice, and walked several miles to the city of Hudson. On reaching the hotel he was at once prostrated with a fever which had begun to develop itself before he left college. It soon assumed a typhoid form; and although attended by skilful physicians and having the watchful care of his parents and other members of his family, he sank under the disease, and died April 12, 1837, in his eighteenth year. He was a youth of peculiarly lovely disposition, of much literary promise, and a sincere, humble Christian, whose great purpose, with the Gospel ministry in view, was to prepare himself for usefulness and to spend his life in the service of his Divine Master.

WILLIAM C. PRIME, LL.D.

WILLIAM COWPER, youngest son of the Rev. Nathaniel S. Prime, D.D., and Julia Ann Jermain, his wife, was born at Cambridge, N.Y., Oct. 31, 1825. He received his early education under the instruction of his father, and entered the Sophomore class in the College of New Jersey (Princeton) in 1840. He was graduated in 1843, and by appointment delivered a poem at the Commencement. Upon leaving college he began the study of law, and was admitted to the Bar of the city of New York in 1846. He continued to practise in the city until the year 1861, when he became one of the owners and managers of the " New York Journal of Commerce," in which he has continued until the present time, having been editor-in-chief from 1861 to 1869. During the years 1855–56, he travelled in Europe and the East, spending most of the time in Egypt and Palestine. Upon his return he published two volumes, " Boat-Life in Egypt and Nubia," and " Tent-Life in the Holy Land," which have had great popularity as sketches of travel and observations on scenes and peoples. His visit to those lands was repeated in the years 1869–70. In both journeys he was accompanied by his wife, Mary Trumbull, daughter of the Hon. Gurdon Trumbull, of Stonington, Conn., whom he married May 1, 1851.

Early in his professional life Mr. Prime adopted the opinion that every man should have some special occupation, apart from his ordinary business in life, by which he might at times completely divert his mind from responsible and exacting labor. He commenced when very young the collection of works of art in various departments, among which for a time he allowed numismatics to occupy his attention. The die-cutter's art led him to the study of engraving; and while pursuing this subject as a historical study, he was directed to a particular department, to which he has devoted himself during the greater part of his life, — the history of the illustration of thought by pictures, as distinct from the history of engraving or of painting, in being confined to the relations between written language and picture-language. His library, in its accumulations for many years, has been specially devoted to this subject, and is rich in early illustrated books and in collections of the woodcuts of artists, known and unknown, of the fifteenth and sixteenth centuries. His publications on this subject have been only in periodicals.

His wife, a lady of rare attainments in literature and art, entered with enthusiasm into his favorite pursuits, devoting herself more especially to the history of pottery and porcelain. The result was the accumulation of the most complete private collection, illustrating the history of the art of pottery, hitherto made in America. This collection will find a permanent place of usefulness in the Art Department of the College of New Jersey at Princeton, to which Mr. Prime has presented it as a memorial of his wife, who died April 3, 1872.

The Metropolitan Museum of Art was founded in the city of New York in 1870, during the absence of Mr. Prime in Europe. Immediately upon his return he took an active interest in the infant institution, the history of which is the history of the devotion of a few private citizens to the instruction and elevation of the popular mind, by promoting an intelligent study of the history of ancient and modern art in all departments, and also by encouraging a successful practice of the finer arts as a pursuit in life. For many years all the responsible labor in the Metropolitan Museum was voluntarily performed by the trustees in person. Down to the present time Mr. Prime has devoted a large part of his time to the interests of this Museum ; and now, in common with his co-trustees, has the satisfaction of witnessing its present magnitude and usefulness, as well as great popularity. He was elected first Vice-President of the Museum in 1874, and has been annually re-elected down to the present time. Schools have been established in connection with the Museum, in which thorough instruction in the arts is given at a trifling expense to the pupils.

Having devoted much time to the study of art history, Mr. Prime became impressed with the importance of introducing in schools and colleges a systematic course of instruction in this department of the history of mankind in all countries and ages. In large measure through his exertions, the Trustees of the College of New Jersey were induced to establish at Princeton such a department, and Mr. Prime presented to the College his extensive and costly ceramic collections, on condition that a fire-proof building, for these and other art collections, should be erected, — a condition which is about to be fulfilled. The venerable President, Dr. McCosh, has taken a deep interest in the matter, and through his laborious advocacy the means have been furnished, and the building is now in process of erection.

In the mean time the department has been organized; and without consulting him, the Trustees of the College in 1884 elected Mr. Prime to the Chair of Professor of the History of Art. Without accepting any responsibility as a member of the Faculty, he has for some years delivered lectures from this Chair.

Princeton College conferred the degree of LL.D. on Mr. Prime in 1875. It is worthy of note that his graduation at this institution presented an instance, then rare in this country, of a young man receiving his degree of A.B. from the college at which his father and grandfather had received it. Benjamin Y. Prime was graduated in 1751, Nathaniel S. Prime in 1804, and William C. Prime in 1843. Two great-great-grandsons of the first (who was a graduate of Yale), both bearing the family name, are now enrolled among the undergraduates at Princeton.

PUBLICATIONS OF WILLIAM C. PRIME, LL.D.

Mr. Prime has been an extensive contributor to the periodical literature of the country in magazines and reviews. In 1846 he commenced a correspondence in the "New York Journal of Commerce," using the signature ꟼꟼ., which became familiar to the readers of that paper. This series has been continued for more than forty years, and is doubtless without a parallel in this respect in the daily Press. Nor is it probable that there is any parallel in the weekly Press, excepting in the celebrated letters of his brother IRENÆUS in the " New York Observer."

THE OWL CREEK LETTERS and Other Correspondence. By W. Baker & Scribner. 1848. pp. 208.

THE OLD HOUSE BY THE RIVER. Harper & Brothers. 1853. pp. 318.

LATER YEARS. Harper & Brothers. 1854. pp. 353.

BOAT LIFE IN EGYPT AND NUBIA. Harper & Brothers. 1857. pp. 498.

TENT LIFE IN THE HOLY LAND. Harper & Brothers. 1857. pp. 498.

COINS, MEDALS, AND SEALS, ANCIENT AND MODERN; Illustrated and Described : With a Sketch of the History of Coins and Coinage ; Instructions for Young Collectors ; Tables of Comparative Rarity ; Price-List of English and American Coins, Medals, and Tokens, etc. [Edited by W. C. Prime.] Harper & Brothers. 1861. pp. 292. 4to.

O MOTHER DEAR, JERUSALEM. The Old Hymn, its Origin and Genealogy. Anson D. F. Randolph. 1865. pp. 112. 12mo.

Same in 4to, illustrated.

INTRODUCTION TO GAUTIER'S ROMANCE OF THE MUMMY. Bradburn. 1863.

I GO A FISHING : Harper & Brothers. 1873. pp. 365.

HOLY CROSS : A History of the Invention, Preservation, and Disappearance of the Wood known as The True Cross : Anson D. F. Randolph & Co. 1877. pp. 143.

POTTERY AND PORCELAIN OF ALL TIMES AND NATIONS; with Tables of Factory and Artists' Marks : for the Use of Collectors. Harper & Brothers. 1878. pp. 531.

In 1886, as literary executor of General George B. McClellan, Dr. Prime edited "MCCLELLAN'S OWN STORY," and wrote for that volume a biographical sketch of the distinguished soldier and statesman.

JAMES B. AND JOHN P. JERMAIN.

THE family record of the Rev. Nathaniel S. Prime, D.D., would not be complete without the names of JAMES BARCLAY and JOHN PIERSON, sons of Sylvanus P. Jermain, of Albany, eldest brother of Mrs. Prime. Their mother having died in their early childhood, they were received into the family of Dr. Prime, in which they were reared and educated. John P. Jermain, the younger, was a warm-hearted, generous youth, with a brilliant mind and high aspirations. He early developed a taste for literary pursuits, and on arriving at manhood established the "Albany Literary Gazette," of which he was editor and manager. But his career was short. He died at Albany, March 10, 1835, at the age of twenty-three.

James B. Jermain was graduated at Amherst College in 1831. He studied law, and commenced practice at Newburgh, N. Y. Nov. 17, 1842, he married Catharine Ann Rice, of Cambridge. After a few years he removed to Albany to assist his father in the management of his large estate, which he inherited on the death of his father in 1869. From that time he has devoted his life, not to the accumulation of property, but largely to the employment of his ample means in works of Christian benevolence. In the year 1873 he erected at Watervliet, N. Y., near his country residence, entirely at his own charges, and at a cost of over $120,000, a church edifice as a memorial of his father, and of his own beloved wife who died April 21, 1873. This church he presented to the Presbytery of Albany, and at the same time guaranteed to that body a fund of $50,000 to be invested for its maintenance.

Chiefly at his own expense, in 1877 he erected " The Home for Aged Men " near the city of Albany. To this institution, besides contributing largely to its current expenses, he has devoted much personal care and attention, seeking to have it made a real home to those who, by reason of age and the loss of property and of friends, have no other.

His only son, Barclay Jermain, a young man of great promise, a graduate of Williams College and a member of the Albany Bar, died July 7, 1882. The following year Mr. Jermain, by the gift of $50,000, founded in his memory the Barclay Jermain Professorship of Moral Philosophy in Williams College, to be filled by the President of the College.

During the past year Mr. Jermain has erected, upon lots provided by the citizens of Albany, a building for the Young Men's Christian Association of that city, which is one of the most substantial and thoroughly equipped buildings for Association work in this country. Seeking advice of those having experience in this department of Christian labor, he has given his attention to the details of construction, and has spared no expense in making it a model building for this purpose. It was dedicated, with appropriate exercises, Sept. 22,

1887, and presented to the Association free of debt. The entire cost of construction, which was wholly assumed by Mr. Jermain, amounted to more than $80,000.

In adding this sketch to the records of the family of Dr. Nathaniel S. Prime, it is proper to say that Mr. Jermain was regarded and treated as a child in his family, and that he has ever cherished toward his foster-parents the veneration and affection of a son. He attributes the formation of his character and his aims to be useful in the world, and especially his efforts to be found faithful as a Christian steward, to the principles instilled into his mind under the parental care and training of Dr. and Mrs. Prime.

PRIME FAMILY LIBRARY.

ONE object which the writer of these Notes had in view in preparing the volume was to set in order, in a form for preservation, a complete bibliographical record of the family to which it is devoted. The literary history of the American branch has been largely given in the biographical sketches which precede this chapter; the putting together of their literary labors has been done in another and a more tangible form.

Some years ago the Rev. Dr. S. Irenæus Prime, who had contributed most voluminously to the catalogue of their published works, conceived the idea of making up a family library, to be composed exclusively of volumes written by those bearing the name of PRIME. He was joined in the undertaking by his brothers, who furnished not only their own works, but such other volumes appropriate to the collection as they had gathered from various sources at home and abroad. It was their purpose, if possible, to make the collection absolutely complete, and to hand it down as an heirloom in the family, to be enlarged by succeeding generations of writers.

It might seem to many an easy task to gather together the publications of a single branch of a single

family, even though extending through two centuries
and many generations. But any one who has noted
how soon a book may drop out of the current of human
thought, and how often, within a score of years or less,
one that has been widely read ceases to be treasured
and apparently passes out of existence, so that a single
copy cannot be found, will not regard the recovery from
oblivion of all the books and pamphlets that have been
named in these Notes a small undertaking.

As a single instance : in the catalogue of the publications of Benjamin Y. Prime, M.D., given in the
sketch of his life, mention is made of a Latin treatise
which he wrote while at the University of Leyden, and
which was the basis of the medical honors he received
at that university. The work was published at Leyden,
and he doubtless brought copies with him to this
country on his return in 1764. But when the collect-
ing of the volumes written by the family was under-
taken, not a single copy of this book was to be found.
It was supposed to have perished, with the main part
of Dr. Prime's medical library, in the Revolutionary
War. The several family collections and family garrets
were searched in vain ; no such book was to be found.
At length a friend who was watching the market for
rare books, and who saw in a London catalogue one
having the name of " Benjaminus Young Prime, A.M.,
" Nov.-Eboracensis Americanus " on the titlepage,
bought it and sent it to the family. It was the desired
volume, and a choice copy, in large quarto, expensively
bound in full calf.

One volume only was now wanting to make the
collection by American authors complete. It was one

of the earlier publications of the Rev. Ebenezer Prime,
printed about the middle of the last century. Its recovery, after so long a time had elapsed since it came
from the press, seemed almost hopeless, and was at length
abandoned. But Dr. S. I. Prime, hearing that a copy
was in the possession of a literary gentleman in New
England, himself an enthusiastic collector of old American books, wrote to him, offering in exchange other
books equally valuable, and even more so to a collector
who would not feel a special interest in its possession
on account of the family name. In pressing this plea
he stated that he had been unable to obtain the book
from any other source, and incautiously admitted that,
so far as he knew, there was not another copy in the
country, if there was one in existence, and that of
course it was essential to the completion of the Prime
collection. On this admission out spoke the spirit of
the genuine antiquarian. He replied that if this was
the only copy extant, neither love nor money would
tempt him to part with it. Not long after, an explora-
tion of the family archives revealed, in a mass of hidden
treasures of the same sort, a copy of the long-looked-for
volume, as good as new, though nearly a century and a
half old.

The library now contains a copy of every book and
important pamphlet known to have emanated from any
member of the family since the settlement of the country. Some of these were published anonymously, and
their authorship was never known to the public, though
the record of their origin had been preserved in family
manuscripts.

But this bibliographical record extends still farther

8

into the past than is indicated by the previous Notes. Among the volumes which compose the collection are two that date back to the days of Queen Elizabeth. They are in English, printed in black-letter, one of them among the finest specimens of this early style of printing the language that can be found at the present day. It confirms the remark often made, that there is no art in which so little improvement has been made as in printing, either in the cutting of movable type or in the press-work. It is an art that had no infancy, no age of rudeness; it seems to have been born perfect.

The volumes referred to were written by the Rev. John Prime, of Oxford University, a friend of Sir Francis Walsingham the astute Foreign Secretary and favorite ambassador of Queen Elizabeth. In the year 1586 the City Council of Oxford established a double lectureship in connection with St. Martin's Church, which was known as the Corporation Church. By an order of the Council the Mayor and Corporation were required, under pains and penalties, to assemble, on the ringing of a bell at an appointed hour, and proceed in a body to this church to attend upon this lecture every Lord's Day morning. This lectureship, which has been continued by municipal authority and patronage to the present day, more than three hundred years, was established by the Council "to further the spread of "Protestant doctrine and to hinder Romanism." Two incumbents were appointed to preach on alternate Sundays. One of the first appointed to the position was the Rev. John Prime, who is spoken of as "a "zealous Calvinist," and who retained the office for many years. One volume in the collection of which we are writing is : —

A ſhort Treatise of the Sacraments generally, & in ſpeciall of Baptiſme & of the Supper. Written by IOHN PRIME, fellowe of Newe Colledge in Oxforde. 1 Cor. 10. 15. *I ſpeak as unto them which haue vnderſtanding ; judge ye what I ſay.* Imprinted at London by Chriſtopher Barker, Printer to the Qeenes moſt Excellent Maiestie, Anno Dom. 1582.

Another volume, published five years later, in black-letter, but much inferior in typographical execution, is :

An Expoſition & Observations Vpon Saint Pavl to the Galatians *debated & Motiues removed*, by IOHN PRIME. At Oxford, Printed by Joseph Barnes, & are to be ſold in Pavls Church-yard, at the ſign of the Tygershead, Anno 1587.

These volumes are strictly Evangelical in doctrine and spirit, and are rich in Scriptural instruction. The Commentary is worthy of republication at the present time. Its antique quaintness of style gives a peculiar charm to its spiritual teachings. We quote the open-ing sentences of the Dedicatory Epistle of the Treatise on the Sacraments, which is addressed to Sir Francis Walsingham, as altogether appropriate to this chapter of Bibliographical Notes.

" The Endeleſſe making of Bookes was a vanitye in " the days of Salomon, when printing was not. The " end of all is the feare of God. Certainly men may " not make it a light matter in conſcience to trouble " the worlde with vnprofitable writinges. Yet as in the

" fhew-bread that was shewed to the people as a figure
" of Christ, the olde loaues hauing serued to their ufe
" were remoued, & other fupplied in their roome, yet
" ftill breade in nature & twelve loaues in nomber;
" fo those writings that figure out Chrift & set foorth
" chrifstian duetye may be oftentimes treated of, &
" eftsoones repeated & added to other mens doinges
" notwithftanding no great variety in the matter or
" maner of handling," etc.

The Rev. John Prime was the author of three other
publications, the titles to which are given below. The
last was printed exactly three hundred years ago.
They are the only volumes or pamphlets known to
have been written by any one bearing the name of
Prime that are not found in this collection.

A Fruitfull Discourse, in 2 Books: the one of Nature,
the other of Grace. Lond.: Tho. Vautrollier. 1583.
12mo.

Sermon, Comparing King Solomon & Queen Elizabeth.
Oxford, 1585.

The Consolations of David briefly applied to Queen
Elizabeth. Oxford: Barnes. 1588. 12mo.

A volume of a later date, to be found in the collection, is an autobiography of George Pryme, Professor
of Political Economy in the University of Cambridge,
England, and Member of Parliament for the borough,
who was born in 1781. The family was Huguenot,
and the descendants cherished the memory and records
of their parentage with enthusiastic ardor. Professor
Pryme in his Reminiscences mentions one of his ances-

tors, a clergyman who had the antiquarian spirit to an intense degree. He wrote of himself: "My zeal for "old MSS., antiquities, and monuments almost eats me "up. I am at very great charges in carrying on my "study, in employing persons at London, Oxford, etc."

One book alone remains to be mentioned, as having a place in this family library not only because it is the Book of books, but on account of its associations. It is a copy of the New Testament in Greek, edited by Professor John Leusden, and printed at Amsterdam in 1740. It was the handbook of the Rev. Ebenezer Prime, the pastor at Huntington, Long Island, in the middle of the last century; it was in use after his death by his son Benjamin Y. Prime, M.D., until *his* death in 1791; it was the text-book in college, and during his long life and ministry, of his son, the Rev. Nathaniel S. Prime, D.D., and afterwards of his son, the Rev. S. Irenæus Prime, D.D., from whom it descended to his son, the Rev. Wendell Prime, D.D., who is now the possessor of the library. It has thus been the manual, in the study of the Word of God in the original Greek, of five generations bearing the name. It has been three times bound.

There is one feature of this library to which we refer with peculiar satisfaction. Although it contains all the permanent publications of the family, there is not a single page in all the books which we would wish to efface. We believe that every one has been written with a sense of responsibility for the proper use of the intellectual powers and acquisitions of the respective authors, and with a conscientious desire to set forth the glory of God and to promote the best interests of mankind. The library is handed down to the coming generations of those who may bear the name, with the injunction that they preserve this feature unmarred; that the leaves of the books that shall in future years be placed upon its shelves — like the leaves of the Tree of Life in the Book of Revelation — may be " for "the healing of the nations."

University Press: John Wilson and Son, Cambridge.

www.ingramcontent.com/pod-product-compliance
Lightning Source LLC
Chambersburg PA
CBHW072202270326
41930CB00011B/2515